Military Expenditure Data in Africa

A Survey of Cameroon, Ethiopia, Ghana, Kenya, Nigeria and Uganda

CU00734501

Stockholm International Peace Research Institute

SIPRI is an independent international institute for research into problems of peace and conflict, especially those of arms control and disarmament. It was established in 1966 to commemorate Sweden's 150 years of unbroken peace.

The Institute is financed mainly by a grant proposed by the Swedish Government. The staff and the Governing Board are international. The Institute also has an Advisory Committee as an international consultative body.

The Governing Board is not responsible for the views expressed in the publications of the Institute.

Governing Board

Ambassador Rolf Ekéus, Chairman (Sweden)
Sir Marrack Goulding, Vice-Chairman (United Kingdom)
Dr Alexei G. Arbatov (Russia)
Dr Willem F. van Eekelen (Netherlands)
Dr Nabil Elaraby (Egypt)
Professor Helga Haftendorn (Germany)
Professor Ronald G. Sutherland (Canada)
The Director

Director

Alyson J. K. Bailes (United Kingdom)

sipri

Stockholm International Peace Research Institute
Signalistgatan 9, SE-169 70 Solna, Sweden
Cable: SIPRI
Telephone: 46 8/655 97 00
Telefax: 46 8/655 97 33
Email: sipri@sipri.org
Internet URL: http://www.sipri.org

Military Expenditure Data in Africa

A Survey of Cameroon, Ethiopia, Ghana, Kenya, Nigeria and Uganda

SIPRI Research Report No. 17

Wuyi Omitoogun

OXFORD UNIVERSITY PRESS
2003

OXFORD

UNIVERSITY PRESS

Great Clarendon Street, Oxford OX2 6DP
Oxford University Press is a department of the University of Oxford.
It furthers the University's objective of excellence in research, scholarship,
and education by publishing worldwide in

Oxford New York
Auckland Bangkok Buenos Aires Cape Town Chennai
Dar es Salaam Delhi Hong Kong Istanbul Karachi Kolkata
Kuala Lumpur Madrid Melbourne Mexico City Mumbai Nairobi
São Paulo Shanghai Taipei Tokyo Toronto

Oxford is a registered trade mark of Oxford University Press
in the UK and certain other countries

Published in the United States
by Oxford University Press Inc., New York

© SIPRI 2003

First published 2003
Reprinted 2004

All rights reserved. No part of this publication may be reproduced,
stored in a retrieval system, or transmitted, in any form or by any means,
without the prior permission in writing of SIPRI or as expressly permitted by law,
or under terms agreed with the appropriate reprographics rights organizations.
Enquiries concerning reproduction outside the scope of the above should be sent to
SIPRI, Signalistgatan 9, SE-169 70 Solna, Sweden

You must not circulate this book in any other binding or cover
and you must impose the same condition on any acquirer

British Library Cataloguing in Publication Data
Data available

Library of Congress Cataloging in Publication Data
Data available

ISBN 0-19-924503-7
ISBN 0-19-924502-9 (*pbk*)

Typeset and originated by Stockholm International Peace Research Institute
Printed in Great Britain on acid-free paper by
Biddles Ltd., King's Lynn, Norfolk

Contents

Preface

This report is the result of a study carried out by Wuyi Omitoogun, Research Associate on the SIPRI Military Expenditure Project, between 1999 and 2001. It examines the quality and the availability of data on military expenditure in a selected group of African states. The main reason for carrying out the study was to determine the reasons for the scarcity of African military expenditure data in the SIPRI database in particular and in the major international sources generally. Interest in African military expenditure grew in the 1990s and the increased demand for reliable information was evidenced by the number of requests SIPRI received from various sources—donors, researchers, students and civil society organizations interested in Africa. The problems which SIPRI, and indeed others, faced in meeting this demand made the present study a necessity.

A major finding of the study is that African states do indeed publish data on military expenditure but that these are rarely given adequate publicity in the countries of origin. Publicity in the media is limited and the circulation of published budget documents is highly restricted. The result is that those who need the data hardly know that they exist or even where to look for them.

This report identifies and discusses the strengths and weaknesses of the various national sources of military expenditure data in the six countries it covers. In particular, it shows that the quality of the data varies from country to country and that a number of factors influence this. Two of the most significant are the influence of donors of economic aid and the general loss of capacity in several countries to compile the necessary statistics. While the influence of donors helps in ensuring that data are produced, their focus on military expenditure and, in some cases, insistence that a certain maximum level of expenditure on defence should not be exceeded encourage the manipulation of data by the countries concerned. The capacity of some of the countries to produce accurate data has been greatly eroded by the loss of highly qualified personnel from the government agencies responsible for gathering data, who have moved to jobs in the more lucrative private sector and the developed world.

The study further shows that to be able to determine the quality of the data from most of these countries it is necessary to have some knowledge of the process or processes of decision making that give rise to the spending level in each case. This is the focus of a second, ongoing SIPRI study which examines the processes of budgeting for the military sector in eight African countries. The present report can thus be seen as a precursor to—and essential reading for—the second study.

Apart from the original and productive research work done by Wuyi Omitoogun, my thanks go to Elisabeth Sköns for her support and leadership; to Petter Stålenheim for his assistance with the database; to Eve Johansson for preparing the manuscript for publication; to Peter Rea for the index; and to all those who assisted Wuyi in all the six countries he visited in the course of his research. He would not have had access to some of the sources but for their help. Funding was provided by the Swedish International Development Cooperation Agency (SIDA).

Alyson J. K. Bailes
Director, SIPRI
July 2003

Acronyms

CFA	Communauté Financière Africaine
DAC	Development Assistance Committee (OECD)
DOD	Department of Defence (Kenya)
DRC	Democratic Republic of the Congo
ECOMOG	Economic Community of West African States (ECOWAS) Monitoring Group
EPRDF	Ethiopian People's Revolutionary Democratic Front
ERP	Economic Recovery Programme (Ghana)
FY	Fiscal year
GDP	Gross domestic product
GFSY	*Government Finance Statistics Yearbook*
IFI	International financial institution
IMF	International Monetary Fund
LDU	Local Defence Unit (Uganda)
MOD	Ministry of Defence
MP	Member of Parliament
MTEF	Medium-Term Expenditure Framework (Ghana, Uganda)
NGO	Non-governmental organization
NRA	National Resistance Army (Uganda)
O&M	Operations and maintenance
ODA	Overseas development assistance
OECD	Organisation for Economic Co-operation and Development
OSCE	Organization for Security and Co-operation in Europe
PNDC	Provisional National Defence Council (Ghana)
R&D	Research and development
SAP	Structural Adjustment Programme
UBOS	Ugandan Bureau of Statistics
UN	United Nations
UNLA	Ugandan National Liberation Army
UPDF	Ugandan People's Defence Forces

1. Introduction

I. Background

Many developing countries do not give high priority to gathering and disseminating basic statistics about their countries. This is the result in part of their lack of the necessary capabilities and in part of a deliberate attempt to provide as limited information as possible to the public and the world at large. In many of these countries data on several key aspects of the state are either unreliable or completely lacking. One of these aspects is the security sector. Many countries regard information in this sector as being sensitive and essential to their national security, and thus avoid providing it—at least in any detail.

While the situation is improving in many countries, it is getting worse in others. Yet information on the security sector is much sought after by a variety of people ranging from donors, researchers and students to humanitarian workers and research and reporting institutions such as the Stockholm International Peace Research Institute (SIPRI).[1]

Impartial data on military expenditure are needed for three main reasons. First, reliable military expenditure data promote democratic discussion of the role and tasks of the military. Second, they facilitate a healthy discussion of resource allocation within the national budget between the military and the civil sectors: reliable data on defence spending show the extent of the resources committed to defence. Third, reliable and standardized data on military expenditure are needed for any discussion between states about meeting their common security needs.[2] In the latter context, good military expenditure data could serve as part of an early-warning system in conflict-prone regions[3] and as a confidence-building measure where states in a particular region or organization agree to share such information between

---

[1] On the international reporting institutions see chapter 2, section III.

[2] United Nations, Reduction of military budgets: objective information on military matters, including transparency of military expenditures, Report of the Secretary-General, UN document A/53/218, 4 Aug. 1998.

[3] On the limited usefulness of military expenditure as an early-warning indicator see Sköns, E. *et al.*, 'Military expenditure and arms production', *SIPRI Yearbook 1998: Armaments, Disarmament and International Security* (Oxford University Press: Oxford, 1998), p. 188.

themselves, as is done within the Organization for Security and Co-operation in Europe (OSCE).[4]

Information on military expenditure has been traditionally important for these reasons, but over the years two new and powerful sources of demand for military expenditure data have emerged. These are: (*a*) the use of transparency in military expenditure as an indicator of good governance, and (*b*) the interest of the donors of development aid in including it as an issue in their dialogue with recipient nations. Critical actors on the international economic and political stage took a renewed interest in military expenditure data after the late 1980s. Specifically, multilateral donors such as the International Monetary Fund (IMF) and the World Bank and other, bilateral donors began to link high military expenditure in developing countries to the widespread deprivation and conflicts in those countries.

The link between resource use, deprivation and conflict made Africa the main (although by no means the only) focus of this renewed interest in military expenditure. In the 12-year period 1990–2001, a total of 19 major armed conflicts occurred in Africa, by far the largest number in any region of the world.[5] The conflicts were as destructive as they were widespread. An estimated 50 million people have died in conflicts in Africa since the majority of the African countries became independent in the 1960s.[6] These conflicts have led to the destruction of infrastructure and underdevelopment of the economy of many of the countries, leading to widespread poverty and misery.

Moreover, war requires the diversion of resources for the purchase of arms and provision for the military. In 1998 United Nations Secretary-General Kofi Annan, in a speech on the causes of conflict and promotion of a durable peace in Africa, called on African countries to reduce their purchases of arms and munitions to below 1.5 per cent of their gross domestic product (GDP) and to commit themselves

---

[4] The obligation on members of the OSCE to report their military expenditure is based on the Vienna Document of 1994. Paragraph 15 of the document includes the rules for reporting military expenditures. Conference on Security and Co-operation in Europe, Vienna Document 1994 of the Negotiations on Confidence- and Security Building Measures, CSCE document 113/94, 28 Nov. 1994.

[5] Eriksson, M., Sollenberg, M. and Wallensteen, P., 'Patterns of major armed conflicts, 1990–2001', *SIPRI Yearbook 2002: Armaments, Disarmament and International Security* (Oxford University Press: Oxford, 2002), p. 65.

[6] Martin, G., 'Conflict resolution, early warning and information exchange', ed. S. Meek, *Controlling Small Arms Proliferation and Reversing Cultures of Violence in Africa and the Indian Ocean*, ISS Monograph series no. 30 (Institute for Security Studies: Pretoria, 1998).

to zero growth in military expenditure for a period of 10 years.[7] This call aroused much interest in the issue of military expenditure and encouraged the search for reliable data for further research on supposedly overspending countries and countries that allocate a disproportionate share of their resources to the military sector. The level of poverty occasioned by the diversion of resources to war also makes Africa a major focus for those who are interested in examining the relationship between military expenditure, war and underdevelopment (or poverty).

On another level, the focus on African military expenditure is a result of the continent's dependence on overseas development assistance (ODA). Of all the regions of the world, Africa receives the largest share of ODA, yet it is the least developed and its people are the most deprived. Between 1995 and 1999 Africa received, on average, 35 per cent of all ODA to the least developed countries.[8] In 1995 this amounted to nearly $22 billion of the more than $59 billion in disbursed ODA, and in 1999 it was more than $15 billion of total disbursed ODA of $51 billion.[9] A number of African states have consistently been among the top 10 recipients of aid and external support generally since independence.[10] Africa has the largest proportion in the world of people living in poverty. According to the World Bank, between 1990 and 1998 the number of people living in poverty in Africa rose from 242 million to 291 million, while the number of those living in absolute poverty (on less than US$1 a day) remained almost unchanged, while in the world as a whole the latter number fell by five percentage points over the same period.[11]

[7] United Nations, The causes of conflict and the promotion of durable peace and sustainable development in Africa, Report of the Secretary-General, UN document A/52/871-S/1998/318, 13 Apr. 1998, p. 7, URL <http://www.un.org/ecosocdev/geninfo/afrec/sgreport/report.htm>. Earlier both the president of the World Bank and the managing director of the IMF had called for specific ceilings on military spending in developing countries. Ball, N., 'Transforming security sectors: the IMF and World Bank approaches', *Conflict, Security and Development*, vol. 1, no. 1 (2001), pp. 45–66.

[8] Organisation for Economic Co-operation and Development (OECD), 'Major recipients of individual DAC members' aid', URL <http://www1.oecd.org/dac/xls/TAB34e.xls>; and OECD, *Development Cooperation: 2000 Report*, vol. 2, no. 1 (2001), pp. 230–33, table 25, 'ODA receipts and selected indicators for developing countries and territories'.

[9] See note 8.

[10] See note 8.

[11] Wolfensohn, J. D., 'Foreword', eds S. Devarajan, D. Dollar and T. Holmgren, *Aid and Reform in Africa: Lessons from Ten Case Studies* (World Bank: Washington, DC, 2001), p. xii.

These two separate but related phenomena make Africa a focus of attention for researchers and policy makers, and this has increased the demand for data on the military expenditure of the African states. The same two phenomena have driven SIPRI's requirements for data, a factor in the choice of case studies for this report.

The demand for and supply of data

The demand for data on African military expenditure cannot be adequately met. This is a problem not only for SIPRI. All the reporting institutions have a major weakness in reporting on the developing countries, especially on Africa with its large number of countries.

The problem exists at two levels: (a) the availability of data, and (b) their quality—reliability and validity.

Generally, the level of *availability* of information on military expenditure in Africa is low. Although some countries do now publish their military expenditure figures, these have usually been aggregate figures of limited value. Military expenditure figures are most useful for policy and research when they are disaggregated into their various components. Moreover, the *reliability* of available data has been questioned in the face of glaring omissions in the published figures. The upshot is that such data have to be used with the utmost caution.

While interest in military expenditure soared, there was no corresponding increase in efforts to develop military expenditure data for the new uses that were emerging for them. Perhaps donors took it for granted that military expenditure data were available and of adequate quality, but this would not appear to be the case. Earlier studies have shown that the quality of data for many countries, especially in the developing world, is low,[12] and many researchers and donors are aware of the limitations of the data available through various sources. Many of the studies and meetings commissioned to address the issue of military expenditure have acknowledged the need for more reliable data for analysis.[13] Yet it would appear that very little effort has been

---

[12] See, e.g., Brzoska, M., 'The reporting of military expenditures', *Journal of Peace Research*, vol. 18, no. 3 (1981), pp. 261–75; and Ball, N., *Third World Security Expenditure: A Statistical Compendium*, FOA Report C 10250-M5 (Swedish National Defence Research Establishment: Stockholm, 1984).

[13] Such meetings include the 1993 expert workshop on military expenditure in developing countries organized by the OECD Development Centre and the 1997 Ottawa Symposium on Military Expenditure in Developing Countries: Security and Development, jointly sponsored by the government of Canada and the OECD Development Assistance Committee (DAC).

devoted by any of the parties concerned—donors, governments and reporting institutions—to improving the quality of the data on which many far-reaching decisions and policy statements are based.

Michael Brzoska and Nicole Ball in their respective studies[14] have identified the various weaknesses inherent in the data provided by the main reporting institutions, especially for developing countries. They have also shown that the major problems with the reporting institutions' data on developing countries' military expenditure are those of the availability and reliability of the primary data. Although Ball was able to analyse 48 developing countries' budget documents and final accounts for a 31-year period (1950–80) on the basis of library research—and concluded that data were indeed available—the reliability of the data was variable. Nor were data available for all countries for the whole of the period she examined.

The level of availability has not improved markedly since Ball published her study almost two decades ago. For many Sub-Saharan African countries the capacity to gather and disseminate vital statistics about their countries has been declining rather than improving over the years. According to the World Bank, 'throughout most of Sub-Saharan Africa during the past 20–30 years, this statistical capacity has eroded and declined, and in the strongest environments has failed to keep pace with growing requirements'.[15] Worse still, the quality of the available information has been further compromised by the reasons for which some developing countries now make the data available—the demand factor. The various ways identified by Ball in which many of them hide the true cost of their military expenditure, either within the budget or off-budget,[16] are still being used and some novel methods have even been added, as this study shows. Ball's conclusion was that it was difficult for the reporting institutions (which are only research institutes), with their limited numbers of staff based in the West, to identify these various means of hiding expenditure without seeing the budget documents or the audited accounts for the countries concerned.

[14] See note 12.
[15] World Bank, 'Statistical capacity and development: concepts and approaches', URL <http://www4.worldbank.org/afr/stats/cap.cfm>.
[16] Ball, N., 'Measuring third world security expenditure: a research note', *World Development*, vol. 12, no. 2 (1984), pp. 157–64.

The IMF and the World Bank are in the best position to identify expenditure given their resources and the access they have to government accounts in the countries they deal with.

The IMF publishes the *Government Finance Statistics Yearbook* (*GFSY*) and the series of Staff Country Reports. The *GFSY* includes government expenditure on defence and other macroeconomic data. These data are used extensively and often uncritically by the reporting institutions, especially for developing countries, because of: (*a*) the comprehensive nature of the IMF definition;[17] and (*b*) the assumption that the IMF's data are credible, as it has the obvious advantage of access to various government accounts. However, empirical evidence suggests that the IMF does not apply its definition of military expenditure consistently. This has been shown elsewhere.[18] Nor is the IMF definition sufficiently comprehensive. Moreover, the IMF has not made adequate use of the opportunity to examine government accounts in order to scrutinize conspicuous military spending, as the case of Kenya shows (see chapter 6). The example of the cost of Zimbabwe's involvement in the war in the Democratic Republic of the Congo (DRC) also buttresses this point.[19] In many instances the IMF data are no better than those available to the reporting institutions.

For a good analysis of developing countries' military expenditure it is essential to go beyond simply analysing a national budget document or final expenditure account. Talking to critical actors in both the budget process and the defence establishment can produce surprising revelations, and that is what this study has done. (Critical actors here include both those responsible for making the budget and those in charge of the policy that dictates what allocation is made to the defence sector.)

[17] For the IMF definition see International Monetary Fund (IMF), *Government Finance Statistics Manual 2001*, 'Annexe to chapter 6: Classification of the functions of government', URL <http://www.imf.org/external/pubs/ft/gfs/manual/index.htm>.

[18] Ball (note 12).

[19] Zimbabwe's expenditure on the war in the DRC completely escaped the scrutiny of the World Bank and IMF officials until they were alerted by a Zimbabwean inside source at one of the ministries. Officials in the Zimbabwean Ministry of Finance and Ministry of Defence had informed the visiting officials that they were spending only US$3 million per month on the war and that the excess, if there was any, was being borne by the government of the DRC. The officials believed this to be true, and on this basis the IMF approved a US$193 million standby credit for Zimbabwe on 2 Aug. 1999. Only when it was alerted to the fact that the amount being spent was in fact several times higher than the figures given did the IMF realize that it had been deceived. Morris, H. and Fidler, S., 'Zimbabwe misled IMF over spending on war', *Financial Times*, 4 Oct. 1999, p. 1.

II. Purpose, scope and method of study

Objectives

The primary objective of this study is to obtain, assess and analyse publicly available data on military expenditure in the most dis-aggregated form possible for a set of African states. Military expenditure data are most useful when broken down into their basic components, whatever the purpose for which the data are required.

There are three interrelated parts to the assessment. The first aim is to understand the *reasons why* data are not available, as a basis for charting the way to obtaining more data, if they exist at all. The second is to examine *how reliable and valid* the data obtained are as a reflection of the total resources devoted to military activities. The third is to identify the various *other channels* through which military activities are funded. An underlying assumption is that an under-standing of the reasons why data are not easily obtainable by reporting institutions will help to elicit a method of correcting the problem and ensuring the steady supply of data. Obtaining more data for these countries will also aid the construction and reconstruction of data series over time for a number of countries in the SIPRI military expenditure database, making for greater consistency.

Scope

This study was originally intended to cover the five-year period 1996–2000 but, because the availability of data for the countries being examined was better than expected, it was extended back in time to start from 1981. This date was chosen because earlier analyses of data on African countries stopped in 1980, and the intervening years would have been left unstudied if this survey had kept to the initial plan.

In terms of geographical coverage, the study is limited to East, Central and West Africa. North and Southern Africa are excluded. In terms of politics and military activities, North Africa is more integrated into the dynamics of Middle East politics and international relations than into those of the rest of Africa and is not well suited for inclusion in the same study as Sub-Saharan African countries. It requires a study of its own. The Southern African countries are not included because (with the probable exception of Angola) data for many of them are already available and are relatively easy to interpret.

The main criteria for the choice of countries were originally: (*a*) the demand for information (this demand also reflects the regional significance of states—their size, population, influence, resources and involvement in conflict[20]); (*b*) the availability of some data; and (*c*) the desire for a broad spread of countries, both geographically and in terms of colonial background. Initially 10 countries were chosen on the basis of these criteria—Cameroon, Ethiopia, Ghana, Kenya, Nigeria, Rwanda, Senegal, Sudan, Tanzania and Uganda. The number was later cut down to six because of a limited project budget and lack of data. Financial difficulties prevented the intended visits to Senegal and Sudan, and lack of resources and time prevented the visit to Tanzania. In the case of Rwanda, the lack of publicly available data was decisive. Thus the six countries covered in this report were those that met the criteria set and from which the author was able to obtain publicly available data.

Methods

Wherever possible, the sources of the data obtained in the respective countries in the course of research for this report are the final audited government accounts. In a few cases estimates from national ministries of finance or defence and offices of statistics have been used. Most of the figures from the national statistics offices are audited accounts.

As far as possible, efforts have been made to clarify 'grey areas' in the documents or the composition of the budget with the help of officers working in the offices from which the documents were obtained, especially in ministries of finance and defence. Needless to say, this has met with varying degrees of success, but the response rate was better than expected. Where clarification was needed, questions were taken up later with some military officers, both retired and serving, whom the author was able to interview in the course of his visits to the countries. They were also more cooperative than anticipated. Persons to be interviewed were chosen by first identifying nationals of the countries concerned who had an interest in military expenditure or security more broadly and could join the SIPRI network of experts. These experts then helped to identify critical internal actors, who spoke at length with the author on various issues in the

---

[20] This is illustrated by the public demand for information from the SIPRI database.

research questions. Some of the insights provided by these inter-viewees are given in the country chapters.

III. Framework of analysis: the issues

The analysis in this study is organized around the three principal issues identified above:

– the availability of data;
– the quality of the available data—their reliability (or accuracy) and validity, that is, whether they are a true representation of what they claim to represent; and
– what military expenditure data include (the composition of data).

The second is the central focus because quality and reliability are central to the utility of data: merely making them available clearly does not satisfy the need for them if their accuracy is not trusted.

The availability of data

Availability is a major problem confronting those using military expenditure data for Africa. Two major factors account for the scarcity of data on military expenditure.

The first is the unwillingness of states to be open about the true cost of their expenditure on their military. States generally regard this information as an official state secret and are wary of revealing it. For African states, as for many other developing countries, withholding information on defence has three main attractions. One is to avoid criticism from within the country about the extent of the resources committed to defence in relation to other sectors, especially health and education. This is particularly true of states whose resources are meagre. A second is the belief that making such information available will be tantamount to opening up the defences of the state to others, especially neighbouring countries—that knowledge of a country's strength will make it vulnerable. The third is that defence, with all the secrecy associated with it, is a fertile source of corruption for those directly in charge of the portfolio.[21]

---

[21] Gupta, S., de Mello, L. and Sharan, R., *Corruption and Military Spending*, IMF Working Paper WP/00/23 (International Monetary Fund: Washington, DC, 2000), URL <http://www.imf.org>.

It follows that, unless they are compelled to do so or unless there are reasons beyond their control, many African states are not willing to make such information available. As one former official put it: 'Who will provide such information, when your friend today can be your enemy tomorrow?'.[22] What he did not add was that those who benefit from the secrecy associated with defence might not want the information released for personal reasons as well.

The second reason for lack of information in the defence sector is the lack of capacity to report exact expenditure on the military. Over the years this capacity has diminished in many African states because they have lost highly qualified professionals from the government service to the better-paid private sector, including several donor projects.[23] Other professionals have migrated abroad within the context of the widely reported brain drain, leaving less qualified and usually less competent officers behind. Where highly qualified individuals are still left they are often too few and far between to make any appreciable impact on the budget process.[24] In such states, the political leaders can then exploit this weakness to siphon off resources by diverting significant amounts of state money to defence, knowing full well that they will not be obliged to account for it.

The reliability of the data

Not only are military expenditure data scarce, but the quality of the data that are available is also very low. The problem of the reliability of the available data emanates from three factors. The first is the unwillingness of states to be open about the true cost of their military establishments—in particular, they hide the actual cost of their investment in arms procurement. Such information is regarded as a state secret. The second is the dearth of qualified staff mentioned above, and the third is the reasons for which data are collected and provided.

This study argues that the nature of the reason that motivates a state to provide military expenditure data largely dictates the quality of the data, and hence their reliability. A state that is compelled by external

---

[22] Personal communication with a former Nigerian director of military intelligence, Accra, Ghana, 8 June 2001.

[23] World Bank, *Can Africa Claim the 21st Century?* (World Bank: Washington, DC, 2000).

[24] Bräutigam, D. L., *Aid Dependence and Governance* (Almqvist & Wiksell International: Stockholm, 2000), p. 42.

actors to provide information will be more inclined to give misleading data than one which provides the data as part of routine government work. A large number of African states are now compelled to publish their military expenditure, either as a result of demands by donors who provide budget support and want evidence of proper accounting or as a result of strong local demand by critical segments of their societies. Others publish the data purely as part of a routine government accounting procedure, and such data are likely to be of better quality, although reduced state capacity may still take its toll.

Reliability alone does not guarantee the *validity* of data if valid data are taken to be data that truly capture the whole of a country's spending on its military's activities. A piece of data may be reliable without being valid. The fact that data emanate from government cannot guarantee their validity, since a government could doctor the data to suit its purposes. The problem of constant changes to the heading under which defence expenditure is budgeted or reported also arises here. A particular item might be listed in one budget under the ministry of defence, in another under a ministry for the armed forces and in yet another under the ministry for security. Sometimes the change will amount to no more than a change in nomenclature; at other times it could involve a significant impact on the composition of the budget. This can greatly affect the validity of data, especially in longitudinal studies. If the composition of data changes repeatedly during the period being studied, a study may not be able to measure adequately what it purports to measure.

The composition of military expenditure

The other issue that forms the kernel of the analysis in this study is that of the *composition* of military expenditure. This is very important for any analysis of military expenditure, especially in studies relating to the relationship between defence and development.

Military expenditure data function best as a measure of the economic resources devoted to defence. To carry out other analyses of military expenditure, such as its relationship with conflict or economic growth, a breakdown of military expenditure into its component parts, for example personnel, operations and maintenance (O&M), procurement (including equipment), and research and development (R&D), is necessary. Most African governments do not provide this sort of breakdown of their military expenditure. Many provide a breakdown of their budget estimates into recurrent and capital costs, but there can be a considerable difference between the breakdown given in the estimates and that given in the final accounts. Yet military expenditure data are most useful when it is possible to identify what the money is buying.

These three issues and an examination of trends and levels of military expenditure in the countries are the primary concerns of this study. In the course of the analysis within the above framework the factors affecting these issues in each country, and by implication the quality of the data, are explained. All the data are presented in a standard (as far as possible) SIPRI format in the appendix, but in each chapter the particular country's peculiarities are explored and explained. The data are also compared with the IMF figures, since most reporting institutions, including SIPRI, use IMF publications (the *GFSY* and country reports) on a regular basis as sources for most developing countries' military expenditure data.

IV. The structure of this book

After this introduction, chapter 2 examines the existing data sources in the context of renewed donor interest in African military expenditure. The following chapters analyse the military expenditure data of the six countries one by one. Chapter 9 compares and summarizes the preceding country studies, and the appendix brings together the various country data in a standard format for easy comparison.

2. Existing data sources

I. Introduction

This chapter gives a general description of the present state of primary sources of data on military expenditure. They can be described on two levels: (*a*) those published by national agencies and international organizations, and (*b*) those published by the international research and reporting institutions.[1] The distinction is important for an appreciation of the volume and quality of data produced within these groups.

II. National and international sources of military expenditure data

There are three main sources within this group. These are: (*a*) national governments; (*b*) the United Nations, of which 191 of the 193 countries of the world are members; and (*c*) the IMF, which has 184 countries as members.

National government sources

All military expenditure data originate ultimately from national governments. Anyone requiring primary data on military expenditure therefore has to go to the main source, the national government. Since national governments own the armed forces on which they expend resources, it follows that only they will have accurate figures on what such expenses amount to. If a national government is unable (whether by commission or by omission) to account accurately for its expenditure on the military, it may be near-impossible for any other source to correct this anomaly, except in the case of very glaring omissions, such as not including the cost of well-known military purchases or activity. Even then, the country could claim that its definition of military expenditure excludes that type of activity or that its purchase was for a force other than the military—for example, the police.

---

[1] On the reporting institutions see section III below.

Table 2.1. African countries which reported their military expenditure to the UN between 1992 and 2002 using the UN Instrument for Reporting Military Expenditures

Country	1992	'93	'94	'95	'96	'97	'98	'99	2000	2001	2002
Burkina Faso	–	–	–	–	–	–	–	–	–	X	–
Madagascar	–	–	X	–	–	–	–	–	X	–	–
Mauritius	–	X	–	–	–	–	–	–	–	–	X
Namibia	–	X	–	–	–	–	–	–	–	–	–
Niger	X	–	–	–	–	–	–	–	–	–	–
Senegal	–	–	–	–	–	–	–	–	–	–	X
Seychelles	–	–	–	–	–	–	–	–	–	–	X
Sierra Leone	–	–	–	–	–	–	–	–	–	–	X
Zimbabwe	–	–	–	–	–	–	–	–	–	–	X
Total	**1**	**2**	**1**	**–**	**–**	**–**	**–**	**–**	**1**	**1**	**5**

– = No return made.

Source: United Nations, Reduction of military budgets: objective information on military matters, including transparency of military expenditures, Report of the Secretary-General (various years).

This type of national peculiarity creates a difficulty for those using military expenditure data as produced by national governments, especially in cross-country analysis. The same problem affects those who advocate a reduction in military expenditure. To guard against this type of national divergence in the definition of military expenditure, the UN initiated the standardized reporting instrument for military expenditure in 1980.

The United Nations reporting instrument

The UN standardized reporting instrument for military expenditure was intended to encourage all the countries of the world to report their military expenditure in a standardized format with a view to facilitating the process of reducing military expenditure worldwide. Later a second objective, of promoting transparency in military budgets and reducing tension worldwide, was added to the original goal. The reporting instrument was thought to be the answer to the problem of national differences in definitions of military expenditure.

However, in spite of the size of the UN's membership and the fact that the General Assembly, which includes all the member states, voted to introduce the reporting instrument, the level of reporting to the UN has been very low. From African governments the response has been abysmally low. Table 2.1 lists the African countries which have reported each year since 1992. Between 1992 and 2002 only 9 of the 53 countries in Africa reported, with a record number of five reporting for 2002. However, several of these countries publish such data at the national level.

Africa is not the only region of the world where countries have not reported regularly to the UN. The reasons given for not reporting include: (*a*) the complex nature of the reporting instrument, (*b*) the incompatibility of the UN matrix with governments' accounting systems, (*c*) the inapplicability of many of the categories in the matrix to national categories of military expenditure, and (*d*) a lack of incentive to report, combined with the existence of several disincentives.[2] Whatever the reasons, the low rate of response to the reporting instrument has denied the users of military expenditure data the opportunity to obtain standardized primary data for many countries which would be ideal for research and policy making.

The *Government Finance Statistics Yearbook*

The IMF is one of the Bretton Woods institutions established after World War II to support post-war reconstruction. Its membership has grown to 184 countries. Its major shareholders, however, remain largely the industrial countries. One of the main services it provides is temporary financial assistance to countries to help ease balance of payments adjustment. By virtue of this role it has come to wield a good deal of influence on numerous countries the world over, and it has direct access to their budget preparations and final accounts through physical examination of these documents and dialogue with the host nation.

The IMF publishes the *GFSY* as part of its policy of providing sound and comparable statistics on the finances of member country governments, asking them to supply information on their national

---

[2] United Nations, Reduction of military budgets: objective information on military matters, including transparency of military expenditures, Report of the Secretary-General, UN document A/53/218, 4 Aug. 1998.

Table 2.2. African countries which included defence expenditure data in their response to the *Government Finance Statistics Yearbook* request for data, 1992–2002[a]

Country	1992	'93	'94	'95	'96	'97	'98	'99	2000	2001	2002
Botswana	X	X	–	X	X	X	X	–	–	–	–
Burkina Faso	X	–	–	X	–	–	–	–	–	–	–
Burundi	–	–	–	–	–	X	X	–	X	–	X
Cameroon	X	–	–	–	X	X	–	–	X	–	–
Congo (DRC)	–	–	X	X	X	–	–	X	–	–	–
Egypt	X	–	X	X	–	X	X	X	–	–	–
Ethiopia	X	X	X	X	X	X	X	–	X	–	X
Gambia	–	–	X	–	–	–	–	–	–	–	–
Ghana	X	–	X	–	–	–	–	–	–	–	–
Guinea-Bissau	X	–	–	–	–	–	–	–	–	–	–
Kenya	X	X	X	–	–	–	X	–	–	–	X
Lesotho	X	–	X	–	X	–	–	–	X	–	–
Liberia	X	–	–	–	–	–	–	–	–	–	–
Madagascar	X	–	–	–	X	X	X	–	–	–	–
Malawi	X	–	–	–	–	–	–	–	–	–	–
Mali	X	–	–	–	–	–	–	–	–	–	–
Mauritius	X	X	X	X	X	X	X	X	X	X	X
Morocco	X	X	–	X	–	–	X	–	–	–	X
Namibia	X	–	–	–	–	–	–	–	–	–	–
Nigeria	X	–	–	–	–	–	–	–	–	–	–
Rwanda	–	–	–	–	–	–	–	–	–	–	–
Seychelles	–	–	–	–	–	X	–	–	X	–	–
Sierra Leone	X	–	–	–	–	–	–	–	–	–	–
South Africa	–	–	–	–	–	–	–	X	–	–	X
Sudan	–	–	–	–	–	–	–	–	–	–	X
Swaziland	X	–	–	–	–	–	–	–	–	–	X
Togo	X	–	–	–	–	–	–	–	–	–	–
Tunisia	X	X	–	–	–	X	–	–	X	–	–
Zambia	–	–	–	–	–	X	X	X	–	–	–
Zimbabwe	X	–	–	–	–	–	–	X	–	–	–
Total	**22**	**6**	**8**	**7**	**7**	**10**	**9**	**6**	**7**	**1**	**8**

– = No return made. DRC = Democratic Republic of the Congo.

[a] When a country repeats the same information as it reported in the previous year without providing any additional or new data, it is not recorded as having reported for the year in question.

Source: International Monetary Fund (IMF), *Government Finance Statistics Yearbook* (IMF: Washington, DC, various editions, 1992–2002).

accounts (including military expenditure) according to a standardized format. The rate of response to these requests is better than that to the UN because the IMF exercises some leverage over governments, especially those which need its facilities.[3] Although its statute forbids interference in countries' political affairs (of which defence is a major part), the IMF does some arm-twisting in such matters from time to time.[4] However, reporting is voluntary. Governments send data for whatever they regard as military expenditure to the *GFSY*. The *GFSY* statistics, like those reported to the UN, are reported in local currency. They include (or governments are asked to include) all categories of government expenditure, and should thus allow easy comparison of defence expenditure with total government expenditure. Table 2.2 shows which African countries included defence expenditure data in their response to the IMF's *GFSY* request for data between 1992 and 2002.

On the whole, the national and international sources of primary data on military expenditure have not provided data as comprehensive as the users of the data would wish. This is in spite of the resources at their disposal and the increased range of uses to which military expenditure data are now being put. The national sources require some standardization at the international level to make them comparable. Unfortunately, attempts at the UN level to achieve this have not been very successful. While the IMF's effort has yielded better results than the UN's, at least in quantitative terms, it could do better considering the resources at its disposal and the singular advantage it enjoys of having access to national accounts (for the Staff Country Reports). In fact, data that are lacking in IMF statistics are to be found in less well-endowed international reporting institutions, in spite of the handicaps they face.

III. The international reporting institutions

The main international reporting institutions are SIPRI in Stockholm, the International Institute for Strategic Studies (IISS) in London, which publishes the annual *The Military Balance*, and the US Bureau

---

[3] United Nations (note 2), p. 8.

[4] Although this is done more often for the Staff Country Reports than for the *GFSY*, increasingly the figures released in the former for most developing countries are identical with those published in the *GFSY*.

of Verification and Compliance, part of the US State Department in Washington, DC, which replaced the former Arms Control and Disarmament Agency (ACDA) in 1999 as a provider of military expenditure data.

The international reporting institutions serve as a bridge between the primary and secondary data sources and the users of the data. They are as much consumers of primary data on military expenditure as they are producers of data. Unlike the IMF and the UN, with their direct access to nearly all national governments, they have to search for military expenditure data from various sources. This is both an asset and a disadvantage.

The IMF and the UN rely on the goodwill of member states to supply them with the necessary data—which may not be forthcoming, as the case of the UN shows, and in the case of the IMF only come in trickles. They cannot publish data unless governments supply them, even if the data are available at the national level. A recent UN report lamented the low rate of response to the reporting instrument given that states themselves are already publishing the data.[5] The international reporting institutions do not have such limitations. They search out and report military expenditure data from various sources, giving preference to data from national governments as the main source or as the basis for estimating a country's military expenditure.

However, lack of access to national governments has its drawbacks. The international reporting institutions have to struggle to get such access in the process of obtaining official military expenditure data. Without any contacts in government, and lacking the status of the IMF or the UN, they are simply ignored by many governments, especially in the developing world. In addition, they lack the financial and human resources to monitor effectively the nearly 200 countries in the world. At SIPRI, for instance, only three researchers work on the military expenditure project, on a very lean budget which does not allow for travel for data collection purposes. Their regular data collection work is done by letter, over the Internet or from newspapers and news journals. In the case of many developing countries which give their budgets only limited publicity, access to such information is foreclosed.

The experience of SIPRI with regard to a developing region such as Africa is illustrative of the frustrations of reporting institutions

<hr>

[5] United Nations (note 2).

engaged in similar work. The SIPRI Military Expenditure Project has been working to improve both the amount of data it collects and the quality of its data set on Africa. While Africa is one of the regions where information is less readily available, demand for data on it is among the highest. This is not surprising given the multitude of conflicts in Africa and the great dependence of many of its countries on external financial support.

Since SIPRI publishes only openly verifiable data, it has developed a questionnaire that is based on its own definition of military expenditure and made as simple as possible. This is sent annually to all countries in the SIPRI database—to ministries of finance and defence, central banks, national statistical offices and sometimes embassies in Stockholm—in an effort to obtain primary data regularly. However, the database still suffers severely from a lack of reliable data on Africa (as well as other regions). The lack of data is reflected in the number of countries on which SIPRI is able to report for the most recent year in the military expenditure tables of the *SIPRI Yearbook*. For instance, in the SIPRI Yearbooks 1994–2003, it was only possible on average to provide data for the most recent years for 16 of the 50 African countries in the SIPRI database. The highest number for any year was 24, recorded for 2002,[6] and the lowest was 8, recorded for 1995.[7]

Many African governments do not take the trouble even to acknowledge receipt of the SIPRI request for data, let alone to complete and return it. Those who complete it one year are not likely to do so the following year (see table 2.3 for a comparison of the rates of response to SIPRI's questionnaire, the UN reporting instrument and the *GFSY*). Only a few countries, such as Mauritius and South Africa, have been consistent in returning the questionnaire, and these are countries that provide data on the Internet in any case. Each year the project struggles to obtain whatever data are available on African countries' military expenditure from whatever sources it can find. Moreover, the data received are usually in aggregate form with no information as to

---

[6] Stålenheim, P. *et al.*, 'Tables of military expenditure', *SIPRI Yearbook 2003: Armaments, Disarmament and International Security* (Oxford University Press: Oxford, 2003), pp. 339–44, table 10A.2, 'Military expenditure by region and country, in local currency, 1993–2002'.

[7] George, P., Bergstrand, B.-G., Clark, S. and Loose-Weintraub, E., 'World military expenditure', *SIPRI Yearbook 1996: Armaments, Disarmament and International Security* (Oxford University Press: Oxford, 1996), pp. 359–64, table 8A.1, 'World military expenditure, in current prices, 1986–95'.

Table 2.3. Responses to SIPRI, UN and IMF requests for military expenditure data, 1992–2002

Figures are numbers of countries.

Year	SIPRI coverage 1	SIPRI requests 2	SIPRI replies[a] 3	UN coverage 4	UN replies[b] 5	IMF coverage 6	IMF replies[c] 7
1992	50	–	–	51	1	52	22
1993	50	–	–	51	2	53	6
1994	50	50	4	52	1	53	8
1995	50	50	–	52	1	53	7
1996	50	50	2	52	–	53	7
1997	50	50	7	52	–	53	10
1998	50	50	7	52	–	53	9
1999	50	50	3	52	–	53	6
2000	50	50	6	52	1	53	7
2001	50	50	5	52	2	53	1
2002	50	50	3	51	5	51	8

IMF = International Monetary Fund.

[a] Benin, Botswana, Burundi, Djibouti, Ghana, Lesotho, Madagascar, Mauritius, Morocco, Mozambique, Namibia, Nigeria, Senegal, Seychelles, South Africa, Swaziland, Tunisia and Uganda.

[b] Burkina Faso, Madagascar, Mauritius, Namibia, Niger, Senegal, Seychelles, Sierra Leone and Zimbabwe.

[c] Botswana, Burkina Faso, Burundi, Cameroon, the Democratic Republic of the Congo (DRC), Egypt, Ethiopia, Gambia, Ghana, Guinea-Bissau, Kenya, Lesotho, Liberia, Madagascar, Malawi, Mali, Mauritius, Morocco, Namibia, Nigeria, Rwanda, Seychelles, Sierra Leone, South Africa, Sudan, Swaziland, Togo, Tunisia, Zambia and Zimbabwe.

what their components are or what definition of military expenditure is used by the country responding. Yet military expenditure data are most useful when they are broken down into their various components, so that the user of the data knows what the expenditure is buying. This information is indispensable to those using military expenditure data for policy and research, many of whom have often arrived at questionable conclusions on the basis of limited military expenditure data available.

Finally, a major shortcoming is that many of the countries whose military expenditure has been reported in the *SIPRI Yearbook* do not have consistent series back in time, as sources of data change frequently. This is partly because some of the established ways of obtaining military expenditure data for other regions have not been effective for Africa or developing countries generally. These include reliance on organizations such as the North Atlantic Treaty Organization (NATO), for data supplied by its members, and on major international organizations such as the IMF, which relies on primary sources, in addition to responses to its own questionnaire.

In order to have comprehensive data on all the regions of the world, including Africa, it is therefore necessary not only to improve existing methods for gathering data on Africa but also to seek an understanding of why military expenditure data on Africa are such a rarity. This book is a first effort to achieve this objective.

3. Cameroon

I. Background

Unlike many African countries, Cameroon has never experienced military rule. Like most of the francophone states, however, it signed a military pact with France at independence, which ensures that the latter is the guarantor of its security,[1] and it remains one of the countries that still preserve such a pact. On the surface, it appears to be independent of its former colonial master. In reality, like all the former French colonies, it is almost totally dependent on France. On at least three different occasions France has had to send in military aid to quell internal dissent that threatened the country's stability.[2] On the economic front as well, France's support has been enormous. The economic downturn experienced by Cameroon from the mid-1980s as a result of the fall in the prices of oil and other commodities, on which the country depended for income, led to increased dependence on France and multilateral agencies for support.

This external dependence, internal unrest, especially in the English-speaking region of Cameroon, and the regular border clashes with its large neighbour, Nigeria, have combined to shape the country's military forces and the cost of maintaining them. Although the defence pact with France still subsists, and normally this should allow the country to have some confidence in its national defence against external aggression, Cameroon cannot be confident of its security. The unease that has characterized its relationship with Nigeria and the crisis over the oil-rich Bakassi Peninsula, which has been disputed with Nigeria since the early 1990s,[3] have ensured that national defence has always been a priority in Cameroon. Its position as a major country in the Central African sub-region also ensures that adequate attention is paid to national defence.

---

[1] Chipman, J., *French Power in Africa* (Basil Blackwell: Oxford, 1989).

[2] Chipman (note 1), pp. 124 and 135.

[3] The International Court of Justice (ICJ) in its ruling on the dispute over the peninsula in Oct. 2002 gave owership of the peninsula to Cameroon, but Nigerian troops and citizens still occupy it. Cameroon and Nigeria are working out the modalities of an amicable resolution to the issues arising from the ICJ judgement, under UN supervision.

The public availability of information on Cameroon's defence sector and economy has in general increased with increased external support.

II. External assistance

From mid-1987 the Government of Cameroon came to rely on external support, especially from the international financial institutions (IFIs), to rescue it from the profound financial difficulties it was experiencing. At about the same time, the increased process of democratization in francophone Africa gave rise to internal agitation for reform, especially in the direction of multiparty democracy. These two factors acting simultaneously impelled the regime of President Paul Biya to make changes to satisfy both constituencies.

It was the pressure from the IFIs that was the more compelling in forcing the regime to become more open. By 1986 Cameroon had begun to experience serious economic hardship, which led to a reduction of its total state budget for fiscal year (FY) 1987/88 by 25 per cent in real terms. The fall in the price of oil and other commodities on which Cameroon relied for revenue was a major cause of the government's dire financial situation. Between 1986 and 1990 overall government spending declined by 48 per cent in real terms, leading to, among other things, serious cutbacks in the salaries and pensions of public-sector workers, while many of them were made to retire prematurely at age 55 as a way of cutting down on public spending.[4] The only public sector salaries that were not affected were those of the armed forces, on which the government depended for protection as the growing financial problems caused popular opposition to grow. By 1988 the government had sought and accepted IMF and World Bank support to the economy in exchange for the introduction of a Structural Adjustment Programme (SAP) and all the accompanying conditionalities.[5]

The IMF and the World Bank became major supporters of Cameroon, and in turn demanded more openness and the repeal of many of the laws hindering the free flow of information. Their involvement

---

[4] van de Walle, N., 'Neopatrimonialism and democracy in Africa, with an illustration from Cameroon', ed. J. Widner, *Economic Change and Political Liberalization in Sub-Saharan Africa* (Johns Hopkins University Press: Baltimore, Md., 1994), pp. 129–57.

[5] van de Walle (note 4).

encouraged a number of other donors, in addition to Cameroon's traditional aid donor, France, to support the government through various aid programmes. While in 1982 Cameroon received only $357 million in aid, by 1994 receipts totalled $643 million[6]—an increase of over 80 per cent in real terms over a period of 12 years—and since then the country has been a major recipient of aid.

It is therefore no accident that the period of increased availability of economic and financial data on Cameroon coincided with the period of greater dependence on external economic assistance. The IFIs' normal requirement of transparency and accountability from aid recipient countries made it mandatory for the government to be more open in its transactions and to make official documents more widely available to more of its people. This was perhaps the main reason for overhauling the process of gathering, publishing and disseminating official statistics in the country.

III. The available official data

The Ministry of Economy and Finance is the main source of national data on social and economic matters in Cameroon. It has various publications that deal with the different aspects of the socio-economic life of the country and nearly all have sections on public finance, where expenditure on different government ministries and agencies is set out. Among these publications are the *Annuaire statistique du Cameroun* (the national statistical yearbook), the *Rapport économique et financier* (the economic and financial report) and the *Loi de finances de la République du Cameroun* (the appropriation act).

While these titles are published regularly every year, they were difficult to find until the late 1990s, when the authorities, in response to pressure from donors, started to make efforts to disseminate them for wider public use. Before this they were not even available in major public libraries. Even the Ministry of Economy and Finance does not have any back copies of the publications in its library. The ministry is aware of the problem and in 2000 began constructing good back series for all the data it had published in order not to lose them completely through lack of proper record keeping. To prevent data being lost in future, it is printing more copies of its publications and keeping

---

[6] Figures are in constant (2000) US dollars. See the appendix, table A1. Except where otherwise stated, figures on military expenditure, government expenditure and other economic data, and their sources are to be found in the appendix.

several copies in its library.[7] The reason for the poor state of record keeping was partly that the circulation of published national statistics was largely restricted to the public officials who used the data in their official capacities and to a very limited circle of private persons. This was the result of a lack both of public interest in the data and of any compelling reason for the government to make data available to the general public beyond simply printing the documents.

The three titles mentioned above are the main national sources of primary data on the military expenditure of Cameroon. All are published by the Ministry of Economy and Finance. However, they often contain different data: this is a function of the purpose of each publication and of when they are published. Table 3.1 illustrates the differences between them.

1. The *Annuaire statistique du Cameroun* is published annually in the third quarter of the year, usually August. It contains data on the socio-economic situation of Cameroon, including government expenditure on defence. It publishes expenditure for five fiscal years, including the current year. However, it does not give a breakdown of the investment budget by ministry. Instead, total government investment expenditure is given in aggregate form.

2. The *Rapport économique et financier* contains data for three years: estimates for the current fiscal year, provisional actual expenditure for the preceding year and actual expenditure for the earliest year covered. Comparisons are provided between the initial estimates for the earliest of the three years covered and actual expenditure, and the degree of variation is shown in a separate column. A comparison is also made between the current fiscal year estimates and the preliminary actuals of the preceding year, with the degree of variation again shown. This is, however, not done consistently in all editions. In some editions figures are given for two years while in others they are for three years, and in some the variation is not given. In the 2000 edition investment expenditure is also broken down by ministry.

3. The *Loi de finances* is the appropriation act as passed by the National Assembly. According to the law guiding the preparation of

---

[7] Interview with Dieder Edoa, Ministry of Economy and Finance, Yaoundé, Oct. 2000.

Table 3.1. A comparison of data on Cameroon's military expenditure from different sources, 1981/82–2000/2001

Figures are in billion Communauté Financière Africaine (CFA) francs and current prices.

Fiscal year[a]	Annuaire statistique	Loi de finances	Rapport économique et financier	GFSY
1981/82	..	23.1	..	..
1982/83	..	27.9	..	52.38
1983/84	..	34.9	..	58.87
1984/85	..	42.1	..	71.31
1985/86	..	48.3	..	60.49
1986/87	..	51.6	..	73.92
1987/88	..	46.4	..	57.45
1988/89	..	45.5	..	47.18
1989/90	..	48.1	..	57.87
1990/91	..	50.1	..	56.40
1991/92	..	50.3	..	53.19
1992/93	..	46.9	51.3	46.92
1993/94	..	48.3	50.3	46.57
1994/95	57.8	56.6	..	64.27
1995/96	57.0	56.7	57.0	..
1996/97	60.8	62.8	62.8	..
1997/98	72.6	75.7	74.3	72.54
1998/99	83.2	86.2	83.2	81.83
1999/2000	..	91.9	..	..
2000/2001	..	83.2	..	..

.. = Not available.

[a] Up to 2002, the Cameroonian fiscal year was different from the calendar year. The figures in this table are therefore not directly comparable with those in the appendix (table A1), which are adjusted to the calendar year.

Sources: Cameroonian Ministry of Economy and Finance, *Annuaire statistique 1997* (Ministry of Economy and Finance: Yaoundé, 1998); Cameroonian Ministry of Economy and Finance, *Loi de finances* (Ministry of Economy and Finance: Yaoundé, various years); Cameroonian Ministry of Economy and Finance, *Rapport économique et financier, 1993/94, 1995/1996 and 1997/98* (Ministry of Economy and Finance: Yaoundé, 1994, 1996 and 1998); and *Government Finance Statistics Yearbook, 1994, 1999* and *2000* (International Monetary Fund: Washington, DC, 1994, 1999 and 2000).

the budget,[8] when the annual budget estimates for the next fiscal year are submitted to the National Assembly for consideration and debate, the final accounts of the fiscal year preceding the current one must be submitted as well. Thus, in principle, the appropriation act as passed should contain the current approved budget and actual expenditure for the previous two fiscal years. The intervening year's final expenditure may or may not be part of the act but it must be part of the following year's draft estimates submitted to the National Assembly.

The breakdown of investment expenditure is given in a separate document called *Budget d'investissement public*, although this is usually difficult to obtain. Apart from the reconstruction of past data initiated in 2000, which includes the disaggregated investment budget for the line ministries since FY 1997/98 to date, the only investment expenditure breakdown that was available to the present author at the National Archives in Yaoundé was for FYs 1985/86 and 1986/87.

The main international source of information on military expenditure on Cameroon is the *Government Finance Statistics Yearbook*.[9]

Comparing the sources

The *Rapport économique et financier* and the *Loi de finances* are the most useful national primary sources for military expenditure data on Cameroon. They provide both estimates for the current year and actual expenditure for the other years. However, as explained above, they cover different numbers of years.

Neither gives any further detail about the composition of the military budget. While some issues of the *Loi de finances* include detailed information on the budget (including a breakdown of investment expenditure), others contain only the allocations to line ministries. Similarly, the new data being reconstructed at the Ministry of Economy and Finance only contain a minimal breakdown into recurrent, personnel and investment expenditures.

The least reliable of the national primary sources is the *Annuaire statistique*. It covers five years—the current year and four preceding

---

[8] Cameroon, Ordinance no. 62 OFF4, 7 Feb. 1962, Article 52, cited in Cameroon, *Budget de l'exercice 1986/1987* [Budget for financial year 1986/87] (Ministry of Economy and Finance: Yaoundé, 1986), p. CIII.

[9] On the *Government Finance Statistics Yearbook* see chapter 1, section I.

years. Ordinarily, the figures for the preceding years would be expected to be actual expenditure and those for the current fiscal year to be estimates, but this is not always the case. Estimates are sometimes given instead of actual expenditure without the status of the figures being specified. In addition, the figures are sometimes only recurrent expenditure, leaving out investment expenditure. This shortcoming becomes glaring when the figures in the *Annuaire statistique* are compared with the figures from the other sources.

The *GFSY* data are supposed to be final expenditure figures. However, this is not true for all years for Cameroon. The *GFSY* is particularly useful for military expenditure data of earlier years, 1980–90. While the *Loi de finances* covered only expenditure figures within the government's annual defence budget for these 10 years, the *GFSY* included expenditure on defence from extra-budgetary accounts as well. These accounts were kept until 1988, when President Biya cancelled them because, according to him, there was no genuine basis for keeping them.[10] For the years when the *GFSY* recorded extra-budgetary spending, 1983–88, its actual expenditure figures for defence were higher than the published figures in the official government publications by 15–36 per cent. However, from 1989 onwards, and especially towards the end of the 1990s, *GFSY* data are less complete. For instance, for FYs 1997/98 and 1998/99 the *GFSY* figures are only recurrent expenditure figures and do not include investment expenditure. This is clear when they are compared with the figures from the *Rapport économique et financier* with a breakdown of defence expenditure into personnel, recurrent and investment expenditure. Nevertheless, the *GFSY* is a useful source of information on Cameroon and its figures are in many cases identical with the final expenditure accounts of the government on defence.

IV. Data quality

Until 1990 there was a secrecy law which prevented government information or material being used until clearance was given for its use. This, coupled with the Mass Communication Law of 1962 and the law on pre-publication censorship of 1983,[11] made the publication

---

[10] Takougang, J. and Krieger, M., *African State and Society in the 1990s: Cameroon's Political Crossroads* (Westview Press: Boulder, Colo., 1998).
[11] Takougang and Krieger (note 10), p. 90.

of government information a risky enterprise. It was difficult to tell exactly when it would constitute an infringement of the law. Punishment for this type of offence ranged from imprisonment for a few months to an indefinite prison term.[12] These laws generally restricted the level of available information on official data.

From the early 1990s, however, this changed thanks to both external and internal pressures on the government.

In terms of reliability, the data for the period prior to 1990 tend to be more accurate given that during this period there were no compelling reasons for the government to falsify data. There was no internal pressure for accountability, since the country was a single-party state until 1990, and the restrictions on freedom of expression and censorship of the press effectively reduced the scope of public complaint on defence expenditure. The volatile relationship with Nigeria and the role of Cameroon in Central Africa could both provide justification enough for any increases in military spending. The government was not dependent on any external assistance before 1986; from independence and until 1986 Cameroon had substantial reserves in the extra-budgetary account,[13] some of which were spent on defence. The annual government publications, however, never included extra-budgetary expenditure broken down by sector. This reflects the limited accountability of the government either to Parliament or to the people. Since there was little external interest in the government accounts there was also no external pressure for accountability. However, accounts must have been kept, since the extra-budgetary spending for 1983–88 was traceable and reported to the *GFSY* for the first time in 1994.

From 1986 onwards the quality of Cameroon's data on military expenditure appears to have changed given the government's reliance on external support and the increasing financial difficulties it faced. From that date onwards the government could only fund about 28 per cent of its investment budget,[14] while a large part of public service salaries could not be paid because of lack of resources. This suggests that even recurrent expenditure could not be met in full. The revenue accruing to the government during this period declined significantly:

[12] Takougang and Krieger (note 10), p. 91.

[13] Ahmadou Ahidjo reportedly left about 300 billion CFA francs in the account on his retirement as president in 1982. Gaillard, P., *Ahmadou Ahidjo, 1922–1989* (Groupe Jeune Afrique: Paris, 1994), p. 183.

[14] van de Walle (note 4), pp. 129–57.

Table 3.2. The composition of Cameroon's military expenditure, 1997/98–2000/2001[a]

Figures are in billion Communauté Financière Africaine (CFA) francs and current prices.

	1997/98	1998/99	1999/2000	2000/2001
Running exp. (personnel)	65.5	75.5	79.4	67.5
Running exp. (services)	7.1	7.6	8.2	10.9
Investment	3.1	3.1	4.3	4.8
Total	**75.7**	**86.2**	**91.9**	**83.2**

[a] Figures for FY 2000/2001 are estimates.

Source: Cameroonian Ministry of Economy and Finance, *Estimates 2000/2001: Public Revenue and Expenditure, 2000* (Ministry of Economy and Finance: Yaoundé, 2000).

by 1991 it was estimated at only 15 per cent of that collected in 1990. Only the security forces were regularly paid.[15]

The 1990s were also a period of unrest and constant skirmishes with Nigeria over the Bakassi Peninsula, with its attendant implications for the cost of maintaining the armed forces and keeping them battle-ready for a possible war against an army as strong and large as that of Nigeria. Thus, it is doubtful whether the figures from the late 1980s reflect the true expenditure on defence or the real burden on the national economy.

By 1994, when the Communauté Financière Africaine (CFA) franc (the common currency of the former French colonies of Africa) was devalued by about 50 per cent, Cameroon was in the midst of domestic unrest and cross-border conflict with Nigeria. These problems made additional demands on the armed forces (and the security agencies as a whole), but the effect on the official defence budget appears to have been insignificant or at best modest. This is unusual for a country engaged in conflict with a much larger adversary.

V. The composition of military expenditure

There are two identifiable parts of the military budget—recurrent and investment expenditure (see table 3.2). The former is divided into

[15] van de Walle (note 4).

personnel costs—wages, salaries and personal emoluments—and services. Typically, personnel account for approximately 90 per cent of the total recurrent expenditure and approximately 85 per cent of the total defence budget. Services (usually for O&M) currently account for approximately 10 per cent of the total running expenses and for 7–8 per cent of the total defence budget.

Investment expenditure is typically 3–5 per cent of the total official defence allocation. This is reportedly not enough to equip the military and is instead usually used for O&M, while major military purchases are made using off-budget sources or extra-budgetary means.[16] The manufacturing by the military of small arms, light weapons and military uniforms also brings in some revenue, which ordinarily should go to the Treasury but which the military have often retained.[17] How much income this brings in is not known, but for the purposes of this study it is sufficient to know that the Cameroon armed forces make additional money that does not go into the national treasury.

VI. Trends in and levels of military expenditure

Military expenditure in Cameroon increased steadily from 1982 to 1986, when the fall in government revenue prompted the introduction of austerity measures. During this five-year period military expenditure increased by 29 per cent. In 1987 and 1988 (the first two of the austerity years) it fell in both nominal and real terms—in 1987 by 14 per cent compared to the previous year, and in 1988 by a further 7.3 per cent, to 20.3 per cent below the 1986 level.[18] However, as a share of government expenditure it increased, showing its continued importance to government even in the midst of economic belt-tightening. Military expenditure continued to be privileged over other items, including health—although still behind education, which, for the most part, remained the highest-spending sector of government.[19]

[16] Edoa (note 7).

[17] Edoa (note 7).

[18] Figures are from the SIPRI database, in calendar years, rather than the Cameroonian fiscal year, calculated on the assumption of an even rate of expenditure throughout the fiscal year. See the appendix, table A1.

[19] Cameroonian Ministry of Economy and Finance, *Loi de finances, 1987* and *Loi de finances, 1988* (Ministry of Economy and Finance: Yaoundé, 1987 and 1988); and *Government Finance Statistics Yearbook, 1994* (International Monetary Fund: Washington, DC, 1994).

For the next three years, 1989–91, military expenditure rose steadily both in real terms and (except in 1991) as a share of government spending—to 8.6 per cent in 1989 and 9.9 per cent in 1990. These years were particularly crucial to the government as it faced serious domestic agitation for change and open border skirmishes with Nigeria (over the Bakassi Peninsula). The rising trend was to continue until 1994, when the share of defence in central government expenditure peaked at 11 per cent.

Between 1995 and 2002 a combination of the devaluation of the CFA franc by approximately 50 per cent and the intensification of the border war with Nigeria ensured an upsurge in military spending in real terms (and nominal terms as well)—from $89 million (at constant 2000 prices) in 1995 to $131 million in 2002, an increase of 47 per cent. In FYs 1994/95–1995/96, military expenditure briefly overtook education as the top government spending priority, primacy being given to the war over Bakassi and the political unrest at home. Education, however, returned to the prime position it had occupied in government spending priority after FY 1996/97.[20]

Notwithstanding the attention paid to defence at this period, official military expenditure as a share of GDP was stable at well under 2 per cent, a share it has maintained over the years from the early 1980s to date. Military spending in Cameroon has thus been responsive to: (*a*) the state of the economy, (*b*) external threats and (*c*) internal unrest, although it would appear that the two latter factors are more significant in determining the trend than the state of the economy.

VII. Summary: assessment of data

Data on public expenditure are becoming increasingly readily available in Cameroon. This is a result of deliberate government effort, supported by donors, to collect and disseminate data about the country for the purposes of planning and development and for public use. Military expenditure data are also being made available as part of this new government effort, although data on defence have always been kept, albeit with limited publicity.

The military expenditure data of Cameroon between 1980 and 1988 can be considered reliable to the extent that they included both

---

[20] International Monetary Fund (IMF), *Government Finance Statistics Yearbook, 1999* (IMF: Washington, DC, 1999).

budgetary and extra-budgetary expenditures and because there was less motivation to manipulate defence expenditure data at this time than there was in later years. Military expenditure data for the subsequent years are less reliable, in particular because of the demands of donors as a major driving force, combined with the border conflict with Nigeria and the existence of known off-budget revenues. These factors, especially the continuing dispute over the Bakassi Peninsula, still apply. The fact that the defence budget is not disaggregated makes it difficult to detect any manipulation of the data. Cameroon has given the increased activity in the disputed peninsula as a major reason for its rising military expenditure.[21] Whether the available official data reflect the totality of its expenses on the military is, however, doubtful.

[21] Cameroonian Ministry of Economy and Finance, *Loi de finance 1999/2000*, URL <http://www.camnet.cm/investir/minfi/loi.htm>.

4. Ethiopia

I. Background

Perhaps because of its history and location, Ethiopia has traditionally set a high premium on its military institutions. Whether under the monarchy (1930–74), the socialist (Derg) regime of Mengistu Haile Mariam (1974–91) or the 'liberal' semi-democratic regime since 1991, the military have always been central to state planning and external relations, and as a result have demanded a significant share of the state's meagre resources. By 1991 the bulk of external loans and grants to Ethiopia were for the military—indeed, about half of its total estimated external debt of over $10 billion is military-related.[1] Its less-than-cordial relations with two contiguous states—Eritrea, against which it fought the 1998–2000 war, and Somalia, a collapsed state—coupled with the increasingly violent internal threat from Ethiopia's largest ethnic group, the Oromo, which is seeking autonomy, will ensure that the military continue to receive significant attention in terms of their role and resources.[2] Irrespective of the regime in power, the influence of the military has remained relatively steady over the years.

Despite a lack of transparency that is characteristic of military-centred governments, data on the military expenditure of Ethiopia are available, even for the socialist period. What may be in doubt is the quality of the available data, given the general suspicion that surrounds the statistics produced by developing countries' government agencies, the generous financing of the military by the Ethiopian Government, and the opposition of many donors (on which the country is highly dependent for support) to lavish spending on a sector that is considered unproductive.

While military-related imports have been responsible for the stock of external debt accumulated by Ethiopia over the years, unfavourable

---

[1] 'Russia writes off US$4.8 bn debt', *Horn of Africa Bulletin*, no. 3 (2001), p. 12. See also Abegaz, B., 'Ethiopia', eds S. Devarajan, D. Dollar and T. Holmgren, *Aid and Reform in Africa: Lessons from Ten Case Studies* (World Bank: Washington, DC, 2001).

[2] The cost of the war with Eritrea is estimated at about 26 billion birr or $2.9 billion. Bhalla, N., 'War "devastated" Ethiopian economy', BBC News online, 7 Aug. 2001, URL <http://news.bbc.co.uk/hi/english/world/africa/newsid_1476000/1476618.stm>; and 'War with Eritrea cost 26 billion birr, expert says', *Daily Monitor* (Addis Ababa), 17 July 2001, URL <http://allafrica.com/stories/200107170056.html>.

climatic conditions and the Derg regime's misguided land policy also contributed significantly to the unhealthy state of the country's finances. Ethiopia has therefore had to rely on external sources for support (military and economic) to meet some of its development objectives and sometimes its basic needs.[3] This gives the donors of aid (economic and military) to the country a good deal of leverage in influencing its direction of policy and public expenditure.

II. External assistance

Ethiopia has always been a major recipient of external aid, both economic and military. Both types have proved vital to it at different times in its chequered history. The strategic location of the country in the Horn of Africa, bounded to the north-east (at least until Eritrea became independent in 1993) by the Red Sea, made it attractive to foreign powers, especially during the cold war. Because it was never really colonized by any power, Ethiopia looked for a big power to guarantee its security, especially after the Italian invasion and occupation of the country between 1936 and 1941.

From the 1940s, but especially from 1953 (when a formal defence agreement was signed) until 1977, the United States was the principal donor of aid to Ethiopia, both economic and military.[4] A 1953 agreement committed the USA to supply weapons to Ethiopia and train the personnel of its armed forces.[5] Between the signing of that agreement and the overthrow of Emperor Haile Selassie in 1974, the USA gave Ethiopia nearly $300 million in military assistance, in addition to supplying most of the weapons it acquired on a grant basis.[6] Economic assistance worth an estimated $350 million was also given by the USA during the same period.[7]

---

[3] On the ratio of external aid to central government expenditure see the appendix, table A2. See also Ethiopian Central Bureau of Statistics, *Statistical Abstract* (Central Bureau of Statistics: Addis Ababa, various years); and National Bank of Ethiopia, *Annual Report* (National Bank of Ethiopia: Addis Ababa, various years).

[4] Lefebvre, J., *Arms for the Horn: US Security Policy in Ethiopia and Somalia 1953–1991* (University of Pittsburgh Press: Pittsburgh, Pa., 1991); and Henze, P. B., *The Horn of Africa: From War to Peace* (Macmillan: London, 1991).

[5] Lefebvre (note 4), pp. 55–74.

[6] Lefebvre (note 4), p. 42.

[7] Brind, H., 'Soviet policy in the Horn of Africa', *International Affairs*, vol. 30 (1984), p. 91.

The Derg regime, which overthrew Haile Selassie in 1974, found Soviet support important for its military pursuits and economic survival.[8] While the USSR provided very little in terms of economic assistance during the regime's 17 years in power, it did according to some sources provide arms worth an estimated $11 billion.[9] Ethiopia also accumulated over $10 billion of debt from the USSR and other donors. Most of its debt to Moscow was for arms imports.[10]

In 1985 Ethiopia received massive flows of aid after the devastating drought and famine that ravaged it in 1984–85. Indeed, this period saw the most rapid inflow of aid to the country: assistance worth over $1.2 billion was given to relieve the suffering of the starving population.[11]

In 1991 the Ethiopian People's Revolutionary Democratic Front (EPRDF) entered Addis Ababa and took over power. Mengistu fled to Zimbabwe. The new transitional government enjoyed great goodwill internationally and attracted support from both bilateral and multilateral donors,[12] and the level of external support has remained high since the overthrow of the Derg regime. In 1988 the overseas development assistance received was 17 per cent of GDP.[13] Over the four years 1991–94, external assistance was over $1 billion per year, on average over 100 per cent of total government expenditure. From 1995 the level dropped but still remained at more than 50 per cent of government spending. The war with Eritrea slowed the flow of aid to less than 33 per cent of government spending, but it has since returned to over 40 per cent on average. However, finding an acceptable level of military expenditure is a major bone of contention between the government and its external supporters. This is in addition to the call for further expansion of the political space in the country to allow for multiparty democracy.

[8] Henze (note 4).

[9] Lefebvre (note 4), p. 42; and Abraham, K., *Ethiopia: From Bullets to the Ballot Box. The Bumpy Road to Democracy and the Political Economy of Transition* (Red Sea Press: Lawrenceville, N.J., 1994).

[10] The exact amount of the debt Ethiopia owed to Russia has been difficult to determine. After negotiations lasting several years, the total was put at about $6 billion, of which 80% was written off by Russia in 2001, while the remaining 20% was taken care of under the debt rescheduling and reduction programme of the Paris Club of creditor countries. 'Russia writes off US$4.8 bn debt' (note 1).

[11] See the appendix, table A2. Except where otherwise stated, figures on military expenditure, government expenditure and other economic data, and their sources are to be found in the appendix.

[12] Abegaz (note 1).

[13] Abraham (note 9).

III. The available official data

Ethiopia compiles statistics on different aspects of the public sector, including defence, and these are available in various publications of government agencies. They include the *Federal Negarit Gazeta* (previously *Negarit Gazeta*); the Central Statistical Authority's *Statistical Abstract*; and the *Annual Reports* of the National Bank of Ethiopia (the central bank). All are available for sale to the public, but the only sales outlets are the organizations that publish the titles. These three are the national primary sources of military expenditure data for Ethiopia.

1. The *Federal Negarit Gazeta*, the official government gazette, publishes the government budget for the year. It provides information on intended government expenditure for one year only. It spells out each ministry's official budget allocation followed by a minor breakdown of the budget by sub-heads. It provides no further detail.

2. The *Statistical Abstract* is published annually and covers different aspects of the socio-economic situation in Ethiopia. Military expenditure data are part of central government expenditure in the Public Finance section, along with data for the other sectors of the economy. The current year's budget figures are published along with (in theory) the actual expenditure figures for the four (sometimes three) previous years. However, in practice this is not always the case. Some of the figures for earlier years may be estimates or at best revised estimates.

Until the 1983 edition, the *Statistical Abstract* also provided a more detailed breakdown than the current and capital expenditure categories. Data were broken down into: (*a*) personnel costs, (*b*) non-personnel costs, *(c)* maintenance and equipment, *(d)* motor vehicles and equipment, (*e*) materials and supplies, and (*f*) current transfers. This type of information, although limited, provides valuable insight into the composition of the military budget of Ethiopia, at least up to 1982/83. From about 1985 to 1989 there was massive recruitment into the army as the war against the EPRDF intensified. This significantly changed the composition of the military budget, but it is not reflected in the *Statistical Abstract*.

3. The *Annual Report* of the National Bank of Ethiopia contains government revenue and expenditure for the current year and the four preceding years by sector. Defence is covered, like any other public

sector, in terms of current budget estimate and actual expenditure of past years and in the current and capital expenditure categories. Unlike the *Statistical Abstract*, the *Annual Report* distinguishes clearly between estimates and actual expenditure. Thus the current year's estimates are designated as such and previous expenditures are shown as actual or preliminary actual figures.

The provision of actual expenditure by the *Annual Report* is of great value, especially when those figures are compared with the budget estimates published by the *Statistical Abstract* or the *Negarit Gazeta*. The difference is considerable in most cases. In addition, the *Annual Report* provides information about the comprehensiveness of the data provided, especially prior to 1991. Specifically, it states that the available data on defence until 1991 did not include extra-budgetary (defence commercial) outlay. These outlays were presumably the commercial arms purchases by the Mengistu regime from the Soviet Union. This is an indication of how reliable the data are as a measure of the resources committed to military activities.

Taken together, these three sources provide a wealth of data on the military expenditure of Ethiopia.

The only standard international source is the annual *Government Finance Statistics Yearbook*.[14] Because the supply of data to the *GFSY* is voluntary, not all countries have their defence expenditure published annually. Ethiopia, however, has a consistent series on defence expenditure in the *GFSY* which goes back to the 1970s. Unfortunately, the series has been inconsistent since approximately 1996.

The *GFSY* figures on Ethiopia's defence expenditure are almost identical with those provided by the National Bank's *Annual Report*. However, whereas the data provided in the *Annual Report* and other internal sources in Ethiopia specifically refer to National Defence as a line head in the government expenditure breakdown, the *GFSY* data refer to General Public Services and Defence in most editions. This creates a problem of separating defence from other services lumped together under that heading. To the extent that the *Annual Report* separates defence from public services, its data are more useful.

---

[14] On the *Government Finance Statistics Yearbook* see chapter 1, section I.

Comparing the sources

The data in the four sources are compared in table 4.1. They are of varying quality. The *Federal Negarit Gazeta*, for instance, only gives information on funds appropriated for one year, by sector (including defence), as approved by Parliament. The *Statistical Abstract*, on the other hand, covers up to a five-year period.

The weakness of the *Statistical Abstract*—that it does not always provide actual expenditure for previous years—has been getting worse year by year. This becomes evident when its figures are compared with those of the National Bank *Annual Report*.

Apart from the problem of not differentiating between actual expenditure and budget estimates, the amount of detail provided in the *Statistical Abstract* has also been on the decline. For instance, as mentioned above, the last time disaggregated defence expenditure data were provided was in the 1982/83 edition (see table 4.2). Before this some form of breakdown of the budget was usually given which, though limited, provided some insight into the categories that were taking the lion's share in the budget.

The main strength of the *Annual Report* lies in its providing actual military expenditure data and its clear indication of the type of data provided, which helps greatly in assessing the actual resources committed to military activities in Ethiopia. Similarly, the information about the non-inclusion of extra-budgetary outlays in the military expenditure data published until 1991 provides some inkling of the comprehensiveness of the data. This makes the *Annual Report* a much better source than the others.

However, it has its own weaknesses. Whereas the *Statistical Abstract* provides disaggregated expenditure figures at least up until 1982/83, the lack of such detail in the *Annual Report* does not allow for much critical scrutiny of the difference between estimates and expenditure. Such a breakdown would have been of great value (especially for the 1980s) in terms of knowing which component of the military budget consumed the bulk of the additional expenditure, in view of the already known fact that personal emoluments take a disproportionate percentage of the military budget.[15]

---

[15] Interview with retired Commodore Mesfin Binega, Addis Ababa, July 2000.

Table 4.1. A comparison of data on Ethiopia's military expenditure from different sources, 1980/81–1999/2000

Figures are in million birr and current prices.

Fiscal year[a]	Federal Negarit Gazeta	Statistical Abstract	Annual Report	GFSY
1980/81	736.8	736.8	736.8	905.4
1981/82	782.5	782.5	782.5	939.8
1982/83	821.2	821.3	821.3	943.4
1983/84	869.6	869.6	869.6	939.1
1984/85	881.7	881.7	881.7	926.4
1985/86	896.8	896.8	896.8	929.4
1986/87	922.1	922.1	1 011.1	1 011.1
1987/88	1 051.1	1 051.1	1 350.7	1 350.7
1988/89	1 494.4	1 494.4	1 654.4	1 674
1989/90	1 741.1	1 741.1	1 841.1	1 956.5
1990/91	..	..	1 646.0	1 768.6
1991/92	681.2	681.2	634	753
1992/93	..	..	680.8	680.8
1993/94	888.5	888.5	663.0	663.0
1994/95	736.7	736.7	736.6	736.6
1995/96	771.6	771.6	771.6	771.6
1996/97	834.8	834.8	834.8	..
1997/98	2 069.8	2 089.5	2 089.5	..
1998/99	2 872.1	2 872.1	..	..
1999/2000	2 500.0	2 500.0	..	..

[a] The Ethiopian fiscal year is different from the calendar year. The figures in this table are therefore not directly comparable to those in the appendix (table A2), which are adjusted to the calendar year.

.. = Not available.

Sources: Ethiopia, *Federal Negarit Gazeta* (Negarit: Addis Ababa, various years); Ethiopian Central Bureau of Statistics, *Statistical Abstract* (Central Bureau of Statistics: Addis Ababa, various years); National Bank of Ethiopia, *Annual Report* (National Bank of Ethiopia: Addis Ababa, various years); and International Monetary Fund (IMF), *Government Finance Statistics Yearbook* (IMF: Washington, DC, various years).

IV. Data quality

Military expenditure data for Ethiopia are available in the national sources described above with long historic series. Their *reliability* is, however, in doubt in view of the propensity of centrally controlled states to manipulate official data. The extensive militarization of Ethiopia over the years in the face of severe poverty may also lend credence to suggestions that the official data, especially on defence, may have been manipulated.

While there is little reason to doubt that this is possible, the likely advantages to be derived from manipulating official data have to be weighed. In the specific case of military expenditure in Ethiopia, why might the government want to manipulate the figures? There are three possible reasons: (*a*) the risk of a domestic outcry over excessive defence spending, (*b*) external pressure from donors, and (*c*) official corruption profiting from the secrecy associated with the defence sector.

1960–89

Over the years, irrespective of the regime in power, Ethiopia has essentially been a closed society with limited access to the outside world and little public access to information. The press is very limited, highly censored and controlled by the government.[16] It is thus very unlikely that the government would want to manipulate defence data in order to satisfy domestic pressure for defence expenditure to be curbed. Second, the volatile nature of the Horn of Africa and the bitter rivalry between Ethiopia and its neighbours suggest that, even if there were a domestic outcry against high defence expenditure, an external justification for it could always be claimed. Third, while Ethiopia's governments over the years may have been dependent on external aid for support, there is little evidence to suggest that there was any pressure from the donors to control expenditure on defence. On the contrary, until 1989 the external military assistance Ethiopia received from a similar range of countries was considerable. Both under the monarchy, when the USA was Ethiopia's main backer, and under the Derg, when the Soviet Union was the main sponsor of the regime, the military component of aid was significant. The issue of the reduction

[16] The Ethiopian Press Law of 1992 ensures that more journalists are arrested and detained in Ethiopia than in any other African country—*c.* 200 over the years. Most of the arrests have been the result of critical comments on government policy. The Ethiopian Free Journalists Association was formed in 1993, but the government did not accord it official recognition until 2000. 'Ethiopia', in *Africa South of the Sahara 2001* (Europa Publications: London, 2000), p. 489.

of military expenditure only became critically important in the donor dialogue with Ethiopia after 1990 and could be a factor in the gradual but steady decline in the level of available data on military expenditure on Ethiopia since then.

It is therefore very unlikely that data on defence prior to 1991 would have been manipulated to suit government purposes. This is not to suggest that they have been accurate. There may have been inaccuracies resulting not from a deliberate attempt to falsify the figures but from lack of capacity—the result of outmoded infrastructure or lack of qualified personnel. A World Bank study in 1987 reported that Ethiopian 'technocrats and civil servants have a reputation for honesty, dedication and competence', in contrast to the experience in many African countries,[17] while more recent World Bank (1997) and IMF (1999) studies found this lack of capacity to be the main weakness of the implementation phase of many of the reform programmes agreed with the country.[18] The Ethiopian Government for its part feels highly frustrated by donors' demands for reform in the face of its glaring capacity limitations.[19] Indeed, as a result of prolonged war and the oppressive nature of the Derg regime, Ethiopia experienced large-scale emigration of skilled manpower to Europe and the USA. For a country with a low literacy level, even by African standards, this could only be expected to affect the state's capacity to perform some of its functions.

It should also be noted that data for the period before 1990, and especially from the more reliable *Annual Report*, were made available only after the defeat of the Derg regime by the new government of Prime Minister Meles Zenawi, which tried to convince the outside world, and especially donors, that the previous regime had spent too much on defence at the expense of other sectors. Other available sources since the end of the Derg regime corroborate some of the data in the *Annual Report*, particularly for the early 1980s.[20] This implies that the data may be reliable to some extent.

[17] World Bank, *Ethiopia: Recent Economic Developments and Prospects for Recovery and Growth* (World Bank: Washington, DC, 1987), p. 3.

[18] World Bank, *Ethiopia: Country Assistance Strategy Paper* (World Bank: Washington, DC, 1997); and International Monetary Fund (IMF), *Ethiopia: Recent Economic Development*, IMF Staff Country Report 98/99 (IMF: Washington, DC, 1999).

[19] Abegaz (note 1), p. 208.

[20] See, e.g., the *GFSY* figures in table 4.1. However, the *GFSY* figures lump together General Public Services and Defence in most editions, while the *Annual Report* separates them. See above in this section.

In essence, therefore, there would appear to have been little incentive to manipulate data on defence before 1991. If there were inaccuracies, they may have resulted from ignorance and lack of proper coordination within the government agencies dealing with the state finances, such as the Ministry of Finance and its defence counterpart, which would take delivery of the military purchases.

Since 1990

The situation has been different since 1990 because of the new international political situation, which does not favour unduly high military expenditure, especially by developing countries dependent on external assistance. Moreover, with the end of the cold war, the IFIs now feel more confident in raising the issue in their dialogue with recipient countries, while countries which need the IFIs' facilities tend to tread cautiously on defence expenditure. In addition, the new openness in Ethiopia has allowed some measure of legitimate opposition which was lacking before and which questions the government's spending pattern. The press is rather freer than it was, although still much restricted by African standards, thus allowing for public scrutiny of government activities; and the plethora of non-governmental organizations (NGOs) working with security issues also scrutinize the government's handling of the security sector and query expenditure on it. All these new developments made the environment in the 1990s quite different from that of the earlier years and provided incentives to manipulate statistics, especially in an area as contentious as military expenditure.

The result has been that in the 1990s, and in particular since 1995, the level of available data has been reducing by the year, and it is now at times difficult to get an up-to-date figure on defence expenditure in Ethiopia. The reason may be associated with the need to exercise caution in the sort of data the government releases, but generally it is believed that the new development has to do with a level of spending on defence that is higher than that approved by donors.[21]

Until 1995 data were made available more readily. The years 1991–95 were the 'honeymoon period' for the new Zenawi regime. The international donors found the regime receptive to most of their

[21] Personal communication, Addis Ababa, June 2000.

demands and wished to help. In particular, they wanted the new regime to cut its military expenditure. The government readily agreed to this because it suited its plan of demobilizing soldiers from the army and some of the EPRDF men who had fought in the war against the Derg regime. Thus, during this period the interests of the donors and the regime coincided, and this facilitated a reduction in military expenditure, an increase in social spending and an increase in the availability of data.[22] From 1996, however, after the initial set of reforms, the need to strengthen the military (which were essentially a guerrilla force being transformed into a standard army) and the emerging strains in relations with Eritrea meant that the regime had to increase military expenditure against the wishes of the donors. From 1996 the available military expenditure data were only budget estimates: actual expenditure was no longer available. The war with Eritrea two years later showed that preparations must have been going on between the two sides for some time, and there is evidence to show that the Ethiopian government probably under-reported its expenditure during the period of preparation.[23]

Military expenditure data in Ethiopia can therefore be divided into two periods for the purposes of examining their reliability and accuracy—the early period, 1960–89, and the period from 1990 to the present. There was little incentive to alter the figures on defence in the early period, and there was little or no local demand for data on military expenditure, so that it was not necessary to manipulate it. By contrast, the 1990s witnessed an unprecedented interest in Ethiopia, a measured increase in general openness in the country and an upsurge in assistance to the new government, which encouraged an internal demand for prudence in the management of the state's resources and a demand for a reduction in less productive expenditure, especially expenditure on defence.

[22] On demobilization see Colletta, N. J., Kostner, M. and Wiederhofer, I., *Case Studies in War-to-Peace Transition: The Demobilization and Reintegration of Ex-Combatants in Ethiopia, Namibia and Uganda*, World Bank Discussion Papers 331 (World Bank: Washington, DC, 1996). Most of the defence data in the National Bank's *Annual Report* were published in the 1990s after the fall of the Derg regime. Earlier editions of the publication contained defence only as part of a highly aggregated category called General Services.

[23] Economist Intelligence Unit (EIU), *Country Report: Ethiopia* (EIU: London, 1st quarter 1999), p. 14.

Table 4.2. The composition of Ethiopia's military expenditure, 1979/80–1982/83[a]

Figures are in million birr and current prices.

Fiscal year	Personnel services	Non-pers. services	Maint., premises and equipment	Motor vehicles and equipment	Material and supplies	Current transfers	Total[b]
1979/80	277.2	41.8	. .	141.2	242.3	47.9	**750.8**
1980/81	279.9	42.2	141.8	12.9	240.7	19.4	**736.8**
1981/82	326.4	48.0	140.2	14.6	232.4	20.9	**782.5**
1982/83	339.1	63.3	147.8	16.7	236.4	21.8	**821.2**

[a] Figures are actual expenditure.

[b] Figures may not add up exactly because of the conventions of rounding.

Source: Ethiopian Central Bureau of Statistics, *Statistical Abstract, 1980, 1981* and *1983* (Central Bureau of Statistics: Addis Ababa, 1981, 1982 and 1984).

V. The composition of military expenditure

There is little doubt that personnel costs are the largest single element in the defence budget (see table 4.2). However, on the basis of the breakdown of previous defence budgets, other items also compete for attention, including procurement, maintenance and supplies. The composition of the military budget suggests that over 60 per cent of the budget currently goes to personnel costs and the rest to routine maintenance, while the main arms purchases are made through special budgets.[24] As a matter of fact, the whole military budget is counted as part of the recurrent expenditure budget.[25]

The actual military expenditure reported in the National Bank's *Annual Report* shows a great discrepancy with the budget estimate figures released by government when the budget is announced. Personnel costs appear to have increased considerably as the war with the EPRDF raged on, especially in the crucial stages between 1988 and early 1990. With the strength of the armed forces increasing by about 30 per cent within this period, the share of the military budget taken by personnel also increased considerably.[26]

[24] Binega (note 15).
[25] Ethiopia, *Federal Negarit Gazeta* (Negarit: Addis Ababa, various years).
[26] Binega (note 15).

VI. Trends in and levels of military expenditure

Ethiopia's military expenditure peaked in 1999 at over $685 million, declining to $406 million (in constant 2000 prices) in 2002.

Before the 1999 peak, military expenditure in Ethiopia had placed a great burden on the economy. In the 1980s, on average it took approximately 38 per cent of central government expenditure and 7.3 per cent of GDP. This disproportionate spending on defence in relation to other sectors was the result of the war against the Eritrean People's Liberation Front (EPLF) and later the EPRDF, which reached its peak between 1989 and 1991, when the Derg regime was defeated. Shortly after, military expenditure declined dramatically both as a share of government expenditure and in real terms. It fell by more than 50 per cent in 1991 on the previous year. By 1995 military expenditure was $99 million (in 2000 prices) or 24 per cent of the 1989 level. As a share of central government expenditure it declined from 41 per cent in 1989 to approximately 8 per cent in 1995 and 1996. This situation was helped greatly by donor support for the demobilization of soldiers begun by the transitional government. This drastically reduced the wage bill and made the new army more manageable.

However, by 1996 military expenditure had started to rise again. The reason for the new increase, it emerged later, was the preparations for the eventual war with Eritrea. Military expenditure rose by 83 per cent in real terms between 1996 and 1997, and by 1998, when the war was under way, it had increased to the 1989 level. By 1999 it was 66 per cent higher, in real terms, than in FY 1989/90 at the peak of the war against the Derg regime.

Although spending started to decline the following year, by 2002 (two years after the war officially ended) military expenditure was still only 1.4 per cent lower in real terms than the 1989 level. As a share of government spending, it increased from the lowest point in 1996 (at 8.2 per cent) to 34.8 per cent in 1999, and by 2002 had only declined to 16 per cent. As a share of GDP, military expenditure was also highest in 1999, at 10.8 per cent, and in 1996 at the lowest level (at 1.9 per cent) over the two decades covered by this study.

The trends in these two decades show a pattern of a peak being reached at the height of conflict. Ethiopia's military expenditure reached an all-time high when the war against the EPRDF was at its fiercest, in FY 1989/90, and the strength of the armed forces was reported to be close to half a million men and women. The war with Eritrea reached its peak in late 1999 and early 2000, just as military expenditure for the year reached a high of 35 per cent of government spending.[27]

Thus, conflict (with hostile neighbours and internal crisis) and the influence of donors, particularly after 1991, have played major roles in determining the level and trend of military expenditure in Ethiopia.

VII. Summary: assessment of data

Military expenditure data are available for Ethiopia in the sources identified, with long time series. However, there is some doubt about their reliability. In assessing data reliability, two distinct periods can be identified—the period of the Derg regime, 1977–90, and the Zenawi era or post-Mengistu period since 1991.

Data for the first period appear to be more reliable than those for the later period. The main reason for this is that data for the period, especially from the more reliable National Bank *Annual Report*, were made available only after the defeat of the Derg regime by the new Zenawi government, which tried to convince the outside world and especially donors that the previous regime had spent too much on defence at the expense of other sectors. In addition, other available sources (especially the *GFSY*) corroborate some of the data in the *Annual Report*, particularly for the early 1980s. This implies that the data may be reliable to some extent.

This does not, however, mean that they are valid. The non-inclusion of extra-budgetary funds (commercial outlays) for defence casts some doubt on the accuracy of the data. Since at the time there was little incentive to manipulate data, this shortcoming may be attributed to a poor accounting system and lack of capacity generally to compile statistics. This is not the case for the later years.

Data for the second period appear to be less reliable, especially after 1996 and the end of the honeymoon period with donors. The fact that actual military expenditure figures for the period 1996–2001 were not made available until after the war with Eritrea casts some doubt on data for the period. First, preparations for the war must have been going on long before the real fighting started in 1998, and the defence budget estimates provided were deliberately understated so that

[27] On the cost of the war with Eritrea see note 2.

Ethiopia could continue to remain in the 'good books' of the donors who insisted on low military expenditure. Second, the influence of the donors is considerable in Ethiopia and their emphasis is on having low military expenditure, to which the government regularly agrees. Prior to the 1998 war the government had agreed to a military expenditure limit of 2–3 per cent of GDP but was not able to stick to it, ostensibly because of the war.[28]

The government has agreed to a fresh limit of 5 per cent of GDP since the end of the war, but in 2002 agreed to refurbish most of its Soviet-made military hardware over a period of years with the support of Russia, at an undisclosed cost.[29] All this creates a large gap between what the government agrees with donors and what it actually does, and by implication casts doubt on the quality of its data.

[28] Economist Intelligence Unit (EIU), *Country Report: Ethiopia* (EIU: London, 3rd quarter 1999), p. 13. See also Economist Intelligence Unit (note 23), p. 14.
[29] 'Russia renewing arms trade with Ethiopia, other African nations', *Vremya MN* (Moscow), 3 Aug. 2002, in Foreign Broadcast Information Service, *Daily Report–Near East and South Asia* (*FBIS-NES*), FBIS-NES-2002-0805, 8 Aug. 2002.

5. Ghana

I. Background

Except for a two-year interregnum in the early 1980s, the military ruled Ghana directly from 1972 until 1992 and indirectly until 2000. Earlier, in 1966, the military had overthrown the civilian government of Kwame Nkrumah and ruled until 1969 when a new constitution ushered in a civilian government. For most of the time while the military were in power, Ghana experienced mixed economic and political fortunes. In the 1980s, under the military regime of Flight-Lieutenant Jerry Rawlings, the country underwent fundamental economic restructuring which stabilized the economy for a time and won general praise from donors as an example of how to reform a battered economy.

The restructuring carried out under the externally supported Economic Recovery Programme (ERP), phases I and II, after 1983 ensured a massive inflow of foreign capital at a level previously unknown in Ghana. Aid to the country increased from approximately $367 million in 1985 to $556 million (in constant 2000 prices) in 1995.[1] This was a massive inflow of capital for a country that was seriously short of foreign exchange, and whose total state budget was the equivalent of $322 million and $941 million (in constant 2000 prices) in 1985 and 1995 respectively. The inflow of capital stabilized the economy, and in particular the currency, the cedi, which had been depreciating rapidly. This brought the military regime a great deal of legitimacy and the leverage to enable it to carry out more reforms. However, it also made the regime totally dependent on, and sensitive to the reactions of, its external sources of support, especially the IMF and the World Bank. Indeed, both phases of the recovery programme were IMF-inspired and the organization remained very active in the life of both the regime and the country throughout the period of the Provisional National Defence Council (PNDC) regime (1981–92) under Rawlings, and even under its civilian successor.

---

[1] See the appendix, table A3. Except where otherwise stated, figures on military expenditure, government expenditure and other economic data, and their sources are to be found in the appendix. See also Tsikata, Y. M., 'Ghana', eds S. Devarajan, D. Dollar and T. Holmgren, *Aid and Reform in Africa: Lessons from Ten Case Studies* (World Bank: Washington, DC, 2001), p. 49.

Since the ability of the military regime to secure more funding depended on meeting the targets and benchmarks set for it by the IFIs, emphasis was placed on producing statistics that were both politically correct and mathematically acceptable but hardly objectively true. The IMF admitted in early 2002 that the former government of Jerry Rawlings had manipulated data to meet targets in order to secure a loan of $100 million.[2] Other studies have also pointed to the manipulation of data by the government in order to present a positive picture of the regime's economic performance so that it would be eligible for more funding.[3] How often the government manipulated the data or in what way—by sector or at the 'macro' level—is not known. The available evidence does not point directly to the manipulation of defence data, although military expenditure is one of the areas most vulnerable to manipulation. Because of the high level of secrecy which surrounded defence issues, and especially military expenditure, under the military regime of Jerry Rawlings and during his first term as a civilian elected president (1992–96), the defence expenditure statistics should be treated with caution.

II. The available official data

Although there are various national sources of data on military expenditure in Ghana, they are not easily available. Two possible reasons can be advanced.

First, for most of the Rawlings military regime in the 1980s and the early 1990s, the defence budget was not public knowledge. This had to do partly with the generally closed nature of the decision-making process under Rawlings until 1995,[4] but also, and more importantly, with the perception that defence issues were secret and that the release of information about them required extra caution. The annual budget statement usually gave only the general thrust of the economy and the policy underpinning it, was always short on specific information, and rarely included allocations to line ministries. On the few occasions

---

[2] 'Ghana "misled" IMF', BBC online, 6 Feb. 2002, URL <http://news.bbc.co.uk/hi/english/business/newsid_1803000/1803198.stm>.

[3] See, e.g., Hutchful, E., *Ghana's Adjustment Experience: The Paradox of Reform* (United Nations Research Institute for Social Development (UNRISD): Geneva, 2002), especially p. 163.

[4] Hutchful, E., 'Military policy and reform in Ghana', *Journal of Modern African Studies*, vol. 35, no. 2 (1997), especially p. 259.

when such details were included, information on the Ministry of Defence (MOD) was so fragmented as to be almost meaningless. This was the practice throughout the 1980s.

Second, when the country returned to democracy in 1992, still under Rawlings but now with a parliament, it was the official policy of parliament never to discuss the defence budget while debating the general budget. This remained the policy until 1995. Indeed, according to the Chairman of the House Committee for Defence in 1994, 'traditionally, Parliament does not debate the Estimates for the Ministry of Defence'.[5] The final defence figure was never disclosed even when the figures for other line ministries were released. The reason given for this was that military expenditure should by nature be kept secret in order not to compromise the country's security.[6] The budget of the MOD was available only to the senior officials of the ministries of finance and defence[7] who were bound by the Official Secrets Act not to disclose the information.[8] While the Ghanaian Statistical Service usually has the figures, this office is not very well known in Ghana and the circulation of the budget document is very limited.

Since 1995, however, the parliament has taken a more active role in discussing all aspects of the budget, including defence and military expenditure, and data are now available in the *Parliamentary Debates*, the parliament's official published proceedings.

The result is that not all the available sources publish regular data on defence. They publish them only when they have access to them, and anyone interested in primary data on national defence spending in Ghana is dependent on different sources in order to put together a consistent time series. This has the obvious disadvantage of mixing estimates and actual expenditure together in a series, with all the drawbacks of this for analysis.

---

[5] Ghanaian Parliament, 'Consideration of annual estimates', *Parliamentary Debates: Official Report*, 4th ser., vol. 4, no. 34 (Graphic Corporation: Accra, 8 Mar. 1994), p. 1332.

[6] Ghanaian Parliament (note 5).

[7] Personal communication, Ministry of Finance, Accra, Mar. 2000. When the present author approached both the Ministry of Finance and the Ministry of Defence for documents relating to the Ministry of Defence budget he was not very successful, especially for the 1980s. Even the Library and Information Department of the Ministry of Finance did not have documents relating to them. He was directed to a director in the ministry, who wanted written permission from either the minister or his deputy before he could help with the request.

[8] Azeem, V. A. and Ahadzie, W., 'Ghana', ed. A. Fölscher, *Budget Transparency and Participation: Five African Case Studies* (Institute for Democracy in South Africa (IDASA): Cape Town, 2002), p. 83.

The sources of primary data on defence spending in Ghana fall into two categories—national and international. The former include the *Parliamentary Debates*; the Appropriation Act; the *Budget Statement and Economic Policy of the Government of Ghana*; the *Medium-Term Expenditure Framework (MTEF) and Annual Estimates (Defence)*; and the *Quarterly Digest of Statistics*. The only standard international source is the *Government Finance Statistics Yearbook*. The value and content of these sources are described below.

1. As part of the annual budget process, the government's expenditure plans are discussed in parliament and the proceedings, like all others, are recorded in the official record, the *Parliamentary Debates*. They report the presentation and discussion of the contents of the defence budget as presented by the minister of defence to parliament like the budgets of other line ministries. The figure for the preceding year is reviewed and questions are put to the minister in order to justify the current estimates. Although some aspects of the discussion are referred to a special committee for debate because of their security implications, the open session is an interesting debate and gives an idea about the state of the Ghanaian armed forces, their role in society and their needs. Sometimes the state of their hardware also features in the debate in parliament.

As mentioned above, the debate on the defence budget by Parliament is a new development and is still evolving. The 2001 edition of the *Parliamentary Debates* included not only a breakdown of military expenditure into recurrent and development expenditure, as in previous editions, but also actual expenditure for the preceding year and an official explanation for the increase in the final figure compared to the estimate approved a year earlier.

2. The Appropriation Act is the law authorizing the use of funds for the purposes stated. This merely states what parliament has already agreed to allocate to the government ministries with a minor breakdown of the allocations. The budget of the MOD is included along with those of other line ministries.

3. The annual *Budget Statement and Economic Policy of the Government of Ghana* contains the government's expenditure plans over the coming months. It does not always break down government expenditure, and when it does it only breaks down defence expenditure into recurrent and development expenditure.

4. *The Medium-Term Expenditure Framework and Annual Estimates* (*MTEF*) *(Defence)* is a new addition to the sources of data on military expenditure in Ghana. The MTEF mode of budgeting started there in 1999. Each line ministry publishes its own MTEF annually, detailing its plans and expected expenditure over the next three years. The expenditures forecast usually do not tally in any respect with what eventually comes in the Budget Statement or Appropriation Act. Nevertheless, the MTEF gives an idea of what is to be expected over the next few years. Although it usually includes expenditure for the preceding year, this is usually an estimate rather than actual expenditure. The MOD does, however, provide some breakdown of the budget (and the targets to be met in other areas over the next two or three years). Here the construction and rehabilitation of barracks currently take a large share of development expenditure.

5. The *Quarterly Digest of Statistics*, published by the Ghanaian Statistical Service, includes military expenditure data in its Public Finance section, along with other line ministries' expenditure figures. Like other publications, it provides the data as recurrent and development expenditure, but it goes a step further by breaking down military expenditure by economic classification, especially for development expenditure. It publishes annual figures for a five-year period, and usually claims that the figures for the four years preceding the current one are actual expenditure. This does not, however, appear to be true in all cases. Some estimates in the Appropriation Act have been reproduced as actual expenditure in the *Quarterly Digest* when other publications such as the *Parliamentary Debates* have published the actual expenditure figures and confirmed these through discussion of their various components.

The IMF *Government Finance Statistics Yearbook* is the only international primary data source on the military expenditure of Ghana.[9] It is important to note that its figures are identical with those in the *Quarterly Digest of Statistics* for the years 1986 and 1988–91, and it is likely that the *Quarterly Digest* is the source for the *GFSY* for those years. However, there have been divergences since 1992. Although the submission of the data is voluntary, Ghana has a good historical series in the *GFSY*, including on defence, at least up to 1993.

Table 5.1 summarizes the data from four of these sources.

---

[9] On the *Government Finance Statistics Yearbook* see chapter 1, section I.

Table 5.1. A comparison of data on Ghana's military expenditure from different sources, 1980–2001

Figures are in million cedis and current prices.

Year	Budget Statement	Parliamentary Debates	Quarterly Digest of Statistics	GFSY
1980	..	..	..	175
1981	..	..	..	488
1982	..	..	..	587
1983	..	..	..	..
1984	..	..	..	1 605
1985	..	..	2 987	3 432
1986	..	..	4 605	4 605
1987	..	..	4 285	6 659
1988	..	..	4 603	4 603
1989	..	..	6 106	6 106
1990	..	..	9 006	9 006
1991	12 598	..	15 230	15 230
1992	..	..	18 201	23 242
1993	..	..	26 600	39 481
1994	..	..	36 147	..
1995	48 066	47 988	58 823	..
1996	..	64 608	87 562	..
1997	..	87 687	..	..
1998	132 812	132 812	..	..
1999	158 060	158 060	..	..
2000	219 330	277 269	..	..
2001	..	231 740	..	..

.. = Not available.

Sources: Ghanaian Government, *Budget Statement and Economic Policy of the Government of Ghana, 1991, 1995, 1998, 1999* and *2000* (Government Publishing Corporation: Accra, various years); Ghanaian Parliament, *Parliamentary Debates, 1995–2001* (Graphic Corporation: Accra, 1995–98 and Department of Official Report: Accra, 1999–2001); Ghanaian Statistical Service, *Quarterly Digest of Statistics* (Ghanaian Statistical Service: Accra, various years); Ghanaian Statistical Service, Personal communication; and International Monetary Fund (IMF), *Government Finance Statistics Yearbook* (IMF: Washington, DC, various years).

Comparing the sources

The *Quarterly Digest of Statistics* appears to be the best of the national sources of data on Ghana's military expenditure. It publishes both current estimates and (although not reliably) actual expenditure figures for the preceding four years. There are, however, three drawbacks. First, the information is not revised every quarter. The figures published throughout the year are the same as the estimates in the budget; they may be reviewed the following year when actual figures are released. This becomes clear when the figures in the latest edition are compared with past editions. Second, sometimes when figures are claimed to be actual expenditure they are the same as the estimates, and this creates a lot of room for doubt. Estimates are sometimes indicated by an asterisk, but when this is not done the user is left wondering whether the figure is an estimate or actual expenditure. This is in part a problem of the auditing agencies in Ghana, but the *Quarterly Digest* should be able to state precisely when the figures are actual expenditure and when they are not, so that the figures can be consistently credible. Third, it does not have a long historical series, as there are no data for the early 1980s.[10]

Its biggest advantage over the other national sources is that it provides a breakdown of military expenditure by economic classification. This gives an idea of how much goes into the purchase or repair of equipment within the armed forces. Another advantage is that it is consistent in its breakdown of the budget into recurrent and development expenditures.

Unlike the *Quarterly Digest of Statistics*, the *Budget Statement* contains only estimates and, as mentioned earlier, expenditure by line ministries is not always broken down. When it is, the breakdown is into the traditional categories of recurrent and development expenditure. Because of this limitation, the *Budget Statement* is not very useful. Nor is it possible to get a historical series because of gaps in the information, especially on military expenditure. This appears to have been a deliberate policy of the Rawlings regime until the beginning of his second term as civilian president in 1996. Thus the budget document rarely contains the expenditure figures for the previous years.

---

[10] At least, the author was unable to obtain the *Quarterly Digest of Statistics* for that period when he visited Accra in Mar. 2000.

The Parliamentary Debates are a fairly good source of data on military expenditure. They contain rich debate on developments in the military sector and a justification for the expenditure being requested by the Ministry of Defence, and provide insight into the needs of the military. The 2001 edition also included a figure for actual military expenditure for the preceding year, which was much higher than the original estimate, and a justification for this increase. Unfortunately the vibrancy of debate is a recent development. The level of debate was not helped by the near-total control of parliament by members of Rawlings' party, which usually rubber-stamped the defence budget without debate or made the case for an increase without much justification.[11] Moreover, for the reasons mentioned above, the *Parliamentary Debates* did not contain military expenditure figures until as recently as 1995—the first year since 1981 in which the defence budget was included in the estimates submitted to Parliament for consideration and discussion.

Although the *GFSY* is not a national source, it has the longest series of all the primary sources. Its figures also appear to be actual expenditure, or at worst revised estimates. The *GFSY* figures are identical with the *Quarterly Digest* figures for 1986 and 1988–91; since 1992 there have been substantial divergences.

III. Data quality

There is a general belief that Ghana's national economic statistics are inaccurate.[12] This is because data are gathered only to satisfy specific purposes, or when they are gathered for the purposes of supporting government development efforts they are usually late and not in tune with reality. The demands for data made by donors of economic assistance when Ghana decided to seek support from the IFIs in the early 1980s put additional pressure on the government, while its capacity for producing the data needed was reduced. The need to meet targets set by the IFIs led to the 'manufacturing' of data which were not empirically true.

---

[11] See, e.g., Ghanaian Parliament, *Parliamentary Debates: Official Report* (Graphic Corporation: Accra), especially 1992–97.

[12] See, e.g., Fine, B. and Boateng, K., 'Labour and employment under structural adjustment', eds E. Aryeetey, J. Harrigan and M. Nissanke, *Economic Reforms in Ghana: The Miracle and the Mirage* (James Currey: Oxford, 2000), especially the section on statistics, pp. 227–28. See also Hutchful (note 4).

While it is now public knowledge that data were indeed manu-
factured or massaged, the specifics of this are still not clear. What is
clear is that, in the light of the secrecy that surrounded the defence
budget for the greater part of the 20 years for which Rawlings ruled
Ghana (first as military ruler and then from 1992 to 2000 as its
civilian president), the likelihood of the defence budget being manipulated, either upwards or downwards, was high. Rawlings was
reported to have been embarrassed by a United Nations Development
Programme (UNDP) report that quoted Ghana as having one of the
lowest levels of military expenditure in Africa. To salvage the situation, he asked a senior official of the Ministry of Finance to issue a
statement to correct that impression.[13] The implication was that the
official concerned should release a much higher figure in order to
disprove the UNDP figure, even if that meant manufacturing the data.

Almost throughout the 1980s, the Ministry of Defence estimates in
the national budget were not made public, and after the return to
democracy in 1992 the new parliament did not discuss the MOD
estimates along with those for other ministries in the national budget
until 1995. It is not surprising, therefore, that there is a general lack of
consistent series on Ghana's military expenditure. Instead, there are
fragmented series from different sources, both national and international.

Moreover, certain revenues accruing to the military (such as the
revenue from peacekeeping missions) are never included in the official data, and these amounts could be substantial since they are paid in
foreign exchange.[14] Even officials at Ghana's Ministry of Finance and
the IMF have admitted that no one can be sure of the exact figures for
Ghana's military expenditure because of this.[15] The extent of the
difference between actual expenditure on defence and budget estimates (see table 5.2) would seem to support such doubts.

For every year for which comparable data exist there seems to be a
huge deviation. In absolute terms it was over 58 billion cedis in 2000.
This is an indication that the sum budgeted was usually an under-
estimate. Given the IFIs' emphasis on the need for fiscal discipline, it
is surprising that such large deviations could occur fairly regularly.
The practice of virement (shifting money from one budget head to

[13] Hutchful (note 4), p. 272.
[14] Hutchful (note 4), p. 270.
[15] Personal communication, Ministry of Finance, Accra, Mar. 2000. See also Hutchful
(note 4).

Table 5.2. Ghana: implementation of military expenditure, 1985–2000
Figures are in million cedis and current prices. Figures in italics are percentages.

Year	Estimate	Actual expenditure	Implementation (%)
1985	2 987	3 432	*115*
1990	4 725	9 006	*211*
1995	48 066	58 823	*122*
2000	219 330	277 269	*126*

Sources: Ghanaian Statistical Service, *Quarterly Digest of Statistics*, vol. 8, no. 4 (1990) and vol. 13, no. 4 (1995); *Government Finance Statistics Yearbook 1990* (International Monetary Fund: Washington, DC, 1991); Ghana, *Budget Statement and Economic Policy of the Government of Ghana* (Ghana Publishing Corporation: Accra, 1995); and Ghanaian Parliament, *Parliamentary Debates 2000* (Department of Official Report: Accra, 2000).

another) is quite common in Ghana and it is not unlikely that money budgeted under other budget heads could have been shifted to accommodate the needs of defence, especially in the early days when security was a major preoccupation of the regime.

On the other hand, it has been suggested that the military and their institutions were neglected over a long period by the government and starved of funds.[16] However, this view is highly contestable given the increases in military expenditure between 1984 and 1987 and the more or less steadily increasing trend between 1991 and 2000.[17]

IV. The composition of military expenditure

The composition of military expenditure in Ghana is not very transparent. Data are disaggregated into recurrent and development expenditure. Recurrent expenditure, consisting of personal emoluments, administration and services, takes 80–90 per cent of the total military budget. Personnel takes a disproportionate share—sometimes as high as 50 per cent—leaving other critical areas such as O&M and capital investment in dire need of resources. The development component of the budget takes whatever is left after recurrent costs have been met. Development expenditure appears to be used for O&M and military

[16] Hutchful (note 4), p. 270.
[17] See section V below.

construction of barracks and other dwellings for armed forces personnel.[18] In essence, therefore, very little is left for the upgrading of equipment and the purchase of other military hardware to enhance military capabilities and readiness.

V. Trends in and levels of military expenditure

Military expenditure in Ghana has been increasing in both nominal and real terms for two decades. The exceptions to this general rise were between 1988 and 1990, when the newly introduced IMF-inspired Structural Adjustment Programme (SAP) demanded cuts in public sector spending and it was expedient for the PNDC government to reduce it; and in 1996 (even though there was a nominal increase of 23 per cent). From 1991 military expenditure started to increase again and has, more or less, maintained the trend over the years since then. The increase in 2000 was the result of an increase in pay and allowances for the armed forces introduced in that year.[19]

Prior to the sharp reduction in spending in 1988, military expenditure had increased by over 100 per cent in real terms between 1984 and 1987. Three reasons may explain these initial substantial increases in military expenditure by the new military regime.

One was the need to redress the perceived neglect of the armed forces by the former military government of General Fredricks Akuffo, which Rawlings and his associates overthrew in 1979 partly because they claimed that the armed forces were being neglected and their budgets reduced. Similar reasons were given when in December 1981 they overthrew the civilian government of Dr Hilla Limann, which they had installed in September 1979: the argument they gave for overthrowing him was the inability of the government to respond effectively to Ghana's problems.[20] It was therefore no surprise that one of the initial tasks of the new regime was to correct the perceived underfunding of the armed forces with an increase of more than 100 per cent in real terms between 1984 and 1987.

---

[18] See, e.g., Ghanaian Parliament, *Parliamentary Debates: Official Report* (Graphic Corporation: Accra, 1995 to 2002); and Ghanaian Ministry of Defence, *The Medium Term Expenditure Framework (MTEF) for 2000–2002 and the Annual Estimates for 2000*, vol. 21 (Ministry of Defence: Accra, 2000).

[19] Ghanaian Parliament, *Parliamentary Debates: Official Report*, 4th series, vol. 28, no. 41 (Graphic Corporation: Accra, 28 Mar. 2001), p. 2952.

[20] Hutchful (note 4), p. 270.

The second reason that could explain why it was possible to increase military expenditure in the early days of the regime in spite of the initial difficulty with resources was the type and nature of reform to which Ghana agreed with the IFIs at the beginning of the ERP in 1983. The initial phase of the ERP (1983–87) emphasized fiscal discipline and the halting of inflation by eliminating deficit financing. The government was able to reduce the deficit by increasing revenue rather than reducing expenditure. More importantly, this first phase of reform 'consisted of reforms that were automatic and involved government declarations rather than detailed implementation' of policy,[21] including the removal of price controls and adjustments in the exchange rate. Only with the next phase of the ERP did the donors become more concerned about public sector management and the lack of a well-coordinated economic policy. By implication, there was still a good deal of room for the government during the first phase of the ERP to increase certain public sector spending, including spending on defence, once the perceived obstacles to obtaining a realistic exchange rate had been removed and inflation had been brought under control.

A third possible justification for the increase in this period was the need to finance the several defence committees set up within the armed forces in the wake of Rawlings' 'revolution' to make the armed forces more democratic and less authoritarian towards the rank and file. This series of committees was unprecedented: every army unit, air force station and naval ship had one and, together with Rawlings' other creations, such as the Armed Forces Sergeant Major, they established a separate and parallel hierarchy of the ranks which, as could be expected, affected discipline and order. The new initiatives would have made additional demands on the resources of the military and may have been catered for in the increased expenditure between 1983 and 1987.

In 1988 the military expenditure of Ghana was reduced by one-half in real terms and, although it began to rise again the following year, the rate of increase was nowhere near that of the initial period after Rawlings and the PNDC came to power. The reduction coincided with the next phase of the ERP, with donor insistence on public sector management reform and better coordination of government economic policy. This phase involved structural adjustment, which placed

[21] Tsikata (note 1), p. 76.

emphasis on reducing public sector spending. It may have been this, combined with the increasing threat which the radical reforms in the armed forces created for the Rawlings regime, that necessitated the cut in military spending—on the one hand satisfying the conditions set by the donors by reducing public spending, and on the other withholding funds from a constituency that was becoming a threat to the regime. It was therefore no surprise that the military soon started to complain about a lack of resources and, as Eboe Hutchful has shown, began to ask the government to make their budget public in order to correct the impression that they were being favoured in terms of budget allocations.[22]

In terms of level of military expenditure as a proportion of total government spending, there has been a fall from the high share of the years 1984–87, when it was on average 6.6 per cent. However, since the beginning of the 1990s the proportion has declined to an average of 3 per cent of government spending. As a share of GDP, defence spending has always been below 1 per cent except for 1985 and 2000, when it was 1 per cent.

VI. Summary: assessment of data

Since the mid-1990s data on the military expenditure of Ghana have become available on a fairly regular basis. However, in constructing a historical series it is still necessary to rely on several sources, as no single source of data has a consistent back series. The *Quarterly Digest of Statistics* is the main national source with the longest time series, but it has not been available since 1997. Nor is it updated quarterly as it should be. Other credible sources of data must therefore serve as alternatives to this fairly reliable source. Here the *Parliamentary Debates* stand out; they also attempt to provide actual expenditure figure of previous allocations to the MOD.

In terms of reliability, the data reflect only expenditure of the MOD and not total expenditure on military activities. The Ghanaian military are known to have received income from their contributions to international peacekeeping forces which is substantial when compared with the military budget. The available data therefore tell only a part of the story.

---

[22] Hutchful (note 4), p. 275.

The secrecy surrounding military budgets until the mid-1990s and the known lack of trust in the nationally published data on Ghana, even in areas that are less sensitive, cast some doubt on the reliability of the data for the period. The discovery by the IMF that Ghana had manipulated data in order to obtain a loan is also testimony to the unreliability of the country's data. However, from 1995 onwards, when parliament started debating and scrutinizing military budgets in the same way as other line ministries' budgets, the data appear to be more reliable, in particular after 2000, when a new government and another political party took over from Rawlings. The presence of a vibrant opposition in parliament in the shape of the party of the former president has ensured more critical debate on budgets generally, and the military budget in particular, which is a sine qua non for reliable data on the country being made available.

6. Kenya

I. Background

In terms of economic resources and population, Kenya is a sub-regional power in East Africa. However, experts on East Africa and within the country believe that it does not invest enough resources (or perhaps does not have enough resources to invest) in its armed forces to match its sub-regional status.[1] Virtually all the countries in the sub-region share borders with Kenya and all, with the exception of Tanzania, have experienced prolonged civil war at different times in the past three decades. However, except for a few exceptional years in the 1970s when the dynamics of regional politics demanded it, Kenya's military expenditure has remained modest and almost unperturbed by the tensions in the sub-region.

Two main reasons can be advanced for this rather atypical pattern. The first is the lack of interest in international politics on the part of the leaders of post-independence Kenya. The first two, Jomo Kenyatta (1961–78) and Daniel Arap Moi (1978–2002), both believed in big-power support to guarantee the security of their country.[2] As a result they established military relationships with both the United States and the United Kingdom. The USA's Rapid Deployment Force is allowed the use of port and onshore facilities in Kenya in exchange for some military assistance and training, while the UK has a small group of military personnel stationed in Kenya and regularly uses Mount Kenya for military exercises.[3] Second, the philosophy of the founding president, Jomo Kenyatta, was that Kenya should maintain only modest and professional armed forces that would guarantee the security of the country and its people from external aggression.[4] That philosophy has continued to be Kenya's guiding principle and would seem to be a factor in the modest growth in the armed forces over the years, despite

---

[1] Pinkney, R., *The International Politics of East Africa* (Manchester University Press: Manchester and New York, 2001), pp. 194 and 198.

[2] 'Kenya', in *Africa South of the Sahara, 1994* (23rd edn) (Europa Publications Ltd: Rochester, 1993), p. 457. See also Pinkney (note 1), p. 143.

[3] *Africa South of the Sahara* (note 2), p. 458; and interviews with Maj.Gen. P. Waweru, Director of Operations and Maintenance, Kenyan Army, and Maj.-Gen. G. M. K. Osmeru, Department of Defence (Systems and Procurement), Nairobi, July 2000.

[4] Karangi, J., 'Budgeting for the military sector: Kenya case study', Draft report for the SIPRI–African Security Dialogue and Research (ASDR) Project on the Military Budgeting Process in Africa, Oct. 2002; and Waweru and Osmeru (note 3).

temptations from the examples of other countries either to intervene in the politics of the sub-continent or to embark on a build-up in response to growing regional tensions.

Against this background it is not surprising that Kenya has maintained a relatively modest military budget. But how modest is it? As with many other African countries, the question remains whether the data on the basis of which judgements are made are reliable. Putting it differently, do official statistics tell the whole story about Kenya's defence expenditure?

II. The available official data

National statistics are available on various aspects of socio-economic development in Kenya. The tradition of producing quantitative data on the country is a long one. It dates back to the early years of independence and has been maintained by the civil service, especially the Central Bureau of Statistics of the Ministry of Finance and Planning. This could be a result of the general need for planning or it could be a function of the need to provide data to the external donors which have been crucial to the macroeconomic stability and policies of Kenya since independence. Whichever is the case, statistics are available on different sectors of the Kenyan economy, including defence. They are equally available in various government publications but relatively expensive to obtain.[5]

There are three national sources of data on military expenditure on Kenya and one international source. The national sources are the *Statistical Abstract* and *Economic Survey* published by the Central Bureau of Statistics, and the *Estimates of Recurrent Expenditure of the Government of Kenya* published by the Government of Kenya (presumably the Ministry of Finance and Planning). All are from the same ministry and there are few discrepancies except in matters of detail and the nature of the data.

1. The *Statistical Abstract* is published annually and contains data for five fiscal years (excluding the year of the title). This gives it the clear advantage of publishing actual expenditure data as opposed to the estimates published by the other sources. It contains data on

---

[5] Kirira, N. and Mwale, S., 'Kenya', ed. A. Fölscher, *Budget Transparency and Participation: Five African Case Studies* (Institute for Democracy in South Africa (IDASA): Cape Town, 2002), p. 127.

defence expenditure in three parts of the section on Public Finance: (*a*) as a line head in aggregated form under Central Government Accounts (Purpose and Economic Analysis); (*b*) under Central Government Accounts categorized by purpose of expenditure, and disaggregated into development and recurrent expenditure; and (*c*) under Central Government Accounts (Economic Analysis of Expenditure, Current Expenditure) as (*i*) Military Construction and Equipment, and (*ii*) Rations and Uniforms (Armed Forces).

2. The *Economic Survey* is published every May before the new budget is announced in June. It aims to give current statistics on Kenya in a timely fashion. Consequently, it provides data for four years including the year of publication. It also highlights the performance of the economy over the previous five years with a focus on the year immediately preceding the year of publication. It provides data on various government main services, including defence, as part of central government expenditure broken down by sector. A breakdown of allocations to all sectors, including defence, into recurrent and development expenditure is also provided.

The figures for the previous year are usually revised estimates while those for the first year are usually actual expenditure. The two intervening years are usually provisional actual expenditure figures. To the extent that the *Survey* provides data for an additional year, which is lacking in the *Abstract*, it is a useful source for current data on military expenditure.

3. The *Estimates of Recurrent Expenditure* provide details of recurrent expenditure for the various government departments, including defence, for the current fiscal year. The Department of Defence (DOD) estimates of recurrent expenditure are disaggregated into salaries and allowances, and other overhead costs. The estimates also give an idea of how much is expected by the DOD in terms of appropriation in aid (see section IV below) or income through its own income-generating activities. Generally figures are given for two years, the current year and the preceding year. The preceding year's figure is the approved estimates while the current year, as would be expected, is the estimates of the DOD.

The international source of data on military expenditure of Kenya is the *Government Finance Statistics Yearbook*.[6]

---

[6] On the *Government Finance Statistics Yearbook* see chapter 1, section I.

Comparing the sources

All the national sources have long historical series that allow for comparison of data from different sources and analysis of trend over time. Since virtually all the available national sources are published by the same body, their figures are similar, differing only in details depending on the purpose and time of each publication. The *Estimates* are useful to the extent that they provide some breakdown of the DOD's current expenditure estimates as well as the approved estimates for the previous year. However, the information they provide on the breakdown of labour costs is of little value as it relates mainly to the civilian staff of the DOD and says nothing about the armed forces. To a great extent, therefore, the *Estimates* are of minimal value apart from providing the estimates for the DOD for the year. These are in any case usually revised significantly later.

The *Economic Survey*, on the other hand, has more useful data on defence. It provides data for four fiscal years (including the year of publication, or current year) divided into recurrent and development expenditure. Usually the figures for the first two years (or, as is often the case, the first year) are actual expenditure while those for the remaining two years are provisional and revised estimates, respectively. Apart from the breakdown into recurrent and development expenditure, there is no further detail on defence expenditure.

The *Statistical Abstract* is perhaps the most useful of the three national sources in terms of defence data. Like the *Economic Survey,* it provides data disaggregated into recurrent and development expenditure. Unlike the *Economic Survey*, however, it is published one fiscal year late. This gives it the advantage of providing actual expenditure figures for most of the years covered. This is not always the case, as some of the data for the previous two fiscal years in some editions are provisional, but these provisional figures are usually the same as the figures later released as actual expenditure. In this sense it can be judged to be a better source than either the *Economic Survey* or the *Estimates*.

Another advantage of the *Statistical Abstract* is that, in the section on economic classification (current expenditure), it identifies military-related components in overall current government expenditure. The identification of military construction and equipment, and rations and uniforms for the armed forces as line items in government current expenditure, is a revelation, as the combined sums allocated to these items annually are high and do not appear to have been counted as part of the allocation to defence. When this is taken into account the defence expenditure of Kenya is much higher than what has been officially reported. This is discussed in greater detail in section III below. The only shortcoming of the *Statistical Abstract* is that it is published one year late.

Their weaknesses notwithstanding, these are very good sources of information on the military expenditure of Kenya. The fact that they are published by government and originate from the same ministry eliminates discrepancies in the figures and eases the task of those searching for data. However, to what extent are the figures a true reflection of total expenditure on the Kenyan armed forces?

III. Data quality

Compared to other African countries, Kenya's official statistics are generally regarded as reliable, if in need of improvement.[7] The fact that all the national sources of statistical information are published by the same ministry and tend to be consistent shows the government's grasp of the essential quantitative data produced by its agencies and ministries. It also creates room for data to be manipulated by the government to suit its purposes if the need arises. However, why might the government want to manipulate the defence figures? Three plausible reasons are: (*a*) to avoid triggering a sub-regional military competition or arms race, (*b*) to prevent a domestic outcry against high military expenditure, and (*c*) to hide the country's true defence expenditure from donors.

On the first of these points, the only time when Kenya had cause to engage in an arms race or a military build-up of any kind was in the mid-1970s, when the regime of President Idi Amin of Uganda embarked on a major military expansion, prompting Kenya to do the same. In 1972 Amin attacked Tanzania. The Kenyan armed forces then embarked on a massive recruitment drive and invested in weapons to keep up with the sub-regional trend[8] and prepare for an

---

[7] Fölscher (note 5), p. 28.

[8] Foltz, W. J., 'The militarization of Africa', eds W. J. Foltz and H. S. Bienen, *Arms and the African: Military Influences on Africa's International Relations* (Yale University Press: New Haven, Conn. and London, 1985), p. 181.

eventual attack by Uganda. Kenya's military expenditure rose from a mere 0.4 per cent of total government spending in fiscal year (FY) 1972/73 to about 8 per cent of government spending in FY 1973/74, when Amin intensified his military build-up.[9] The recruitment and weapon procurement programmes turned out to be greater than was actually needed, and have been responsible for the enlarged armed forces Kenya has today.[10] Since then the government has reverted to its old philosophy of maintaining a small but professional military and modest defence expenditure, placing an embargo on the recruitment of new personnel and not replacing those who leave the service. Given the volatile nature of relations within the East African sub-region and tensions at Kenya's borders with virtually all the neighbouring countries over the years, an obvious increase in its military expenditure and procurement might trigger a repeat of the early and late 1970s in the sub-region, which Kenya might not want.

Official under-reporting of data on defence in order to make them look modest would make obvious sense in this context.

The second possible reason that could lead to under-reporting of military expenditure is to prevent a domestic outcry over government spending patterns. Before 1992, Kenya was a one-party state where no official opposition party was allowed, and the media were highly censored. The Public Security Act 1966 ensured that any suspect could be held without trial and seditious publications muzzled.[11] Beginning with the first president, Jomo Kenyatta, and intensifying under President Arap Moi up to 2002, there was zero tolerance for opposition. In effect public criticism of government activities was strictly confined to well-known politicians such as Odinga Odinga, who repeatedly criticized the government, especially from the 1980s, for signing the military pact with the USA which allowed the latter the use of military facilities in Kenya.[12] In addition, the Official Secrets Act prohibits officials from releasing confidential information.

[9] Kenyan Government, *Estimates of Recurrent Expenditure, 1971/72* (Government Printer: Nairobi, 1971); and *Estimates of Recurrent Expenditure, 1973/74* (Government Printer: Nairobi, 1973).

[10] Waweru and Osmeru (note 3). See also Foltz (note 8), p. 181.

[11] Although multiparty democracy was introduced to Kenya in 1992, legislation ending detention without trial, granting freedom of association and repealing the sedition law was passed in Parliament only in 1997 and the constitution was amended to reflect the new changes. However, government harassment of the press and opposition parties continued unabated.

[12] *Africa South of the Sahara* (note 2), p. 453.

Essentially, government spending was not open to criticism and it would have been unwise to be critical about defence issues in any case, especially after the attempted coup of 1982, when the government attributed every word of dissent or criticism to sympathy for the coup plotters.[13] Long prison sentences were the penalty for such an offence. Thus, if the government was spending more than necessary on defence and was concerned about public opinion, sources of internal opposition had already been muzzled and the government did not need to manipulate figures to suit its purpose. Moreover, the highly unstable situation in most of the countries in the sub-region and the constant border clashes would have been enough to justify high military expenditure if justification were needed. In addition, the international system was still tolerant of high military expenditure until the end of the cold war in 1989.

The third possible reason why the government might want to manipulate the defence expenditure figures is the conditions set by donors requiring modest allocations to defence. Over the 20 years 1981–2000 Kenya received overseas development assistance totalling more than $15 billion.[14] At the peak in 1989–90, net aid inflows were equivalent to 31 per cent of the government budget.[15] This was a major source of leverage over the country for donors.

In the past two decades international donors, led by the IMF and the World Bank, have been crucial in instigating important political changes in Kenya by virtue of their leverage over the country. They were instrumental in the introduction of multiparty democracy in the country in the early 1990s, and since 1998 have suspended all facilities to Kenya pending implementation of public sector reforms to promote good governance.[16] However, Kenya's military expenditure as such has never become a source of concern for its donors—at least not publicly—as it has been with other countries, such as Tanzania and Uganda. Over the years the core issue has rather been that of

---

[13] *Africa South of the Sahara* (note 2), p. 610. There have been some positive changes since Jan. 2003.

[14] See the appendix, table A4. Except where otherwise stated, figures on military expenditure, government expenditure and other economic data, and their sources are to be found in the appendix. See also O'Brien, F. S. and Ryan, T. C. I. M., 'Kenya', eds S. Devarajan, D. Dollar and T. Holmgren, *Aid and Reform in Africa: Lessons from Ten Case Studies* (World Bank: Washington, DC, 2001), p. 514.

[15] See also O'Brien and Ryan (note 14), p. 471.

[16] Brown, S., 'Authoritarian leaders and multiparty elections in Africa: how foreign donors help to keep Kenya's Daniel Arap Moi in power', *Third World Quarterly*, vol. 22, no. 5 (2001), pp. 725–39.

Table 6.1. The military expenditure of Kenya: total, and military construction and equipment, 1980/81–1996/97

Figures are in million Kenyan shillings and current prices. Figures in italics are percentages.

Fiscal year[a]	Military construction and equipment	Military expenditure	Military construction and equipment as % of military expenditure
1980/81	1 607	1 795	*89.5*
1981/82	2 290	2 269	*89.1*
1982/83	2 457	2 755	*89.2*
1983/84	2 504	2 801	*89.4*
1984/85	1 980	2 244	*88.2*
1985/86	2 285	2 546	*89.7*
1986/87	3 004	3 335	*90.1*
1987/88	4 386	4 886	*89.8*
1988/89	3 626	4 021	*90.2*
1989/90	4 824	5 385	*89.6*
1990/91	5 308	5 910	*89.8*
1991/92	4 168	4 648	*89.7*
1992/93	4 843	5 406	*89.6*
1993/94	6 094	6 856	*88.9*
1994/95	5 637	6 297	*89.5*
1995/96	8 022	9 039	*88.7*
1996/97	9 285	10 472	*88.7*

[a] The Kenyan fiscal year runs from Apr. to Mar. The figures in this table are therefore not directly comparable to those in the appendix (table A4), which are adjusted to the calendar year.

Source: Kenyan Central Bureau of Statistics, *Statistical Abstract* (Central Bureau of Statistics: Nairobi, various years).

governance—political freedom, accountability and transparency in government. Essentially, therefore, Kenya is not likely to have attempted to hide its military expenditure figures because of pressure from the donors.

The focus should therefore not be on the possibility of data being manipulated so much as on the question whether the data on defence actually reflect the totality of expenditure on the military.

A significant proportion of Kenya's military expenditure does appear not to have been counted as part of the official military expenditure reported over the years, thus casting doubt on the available official data.[17] When the *Statistical Abstract* is seriously scrutinized, more seems to be allocated to defence than is reported under the Defence budget head. The section on Military Construction and Equipment, explicitly described as military (as opposed to other categories in the same section, such as that called Maintenance of Plant, Machinery, Equipment, Buildings Etc.), is clearly meant to be different from non-military categories. For the amounts reported in this section of the *Statistical Abstract*, see table 6.1. Between 1980/81 and 1996/97 the figures ranged between 88 and 90 per cent of the total allocation to defence (see table 6.1).

If the allocations to Military Construction and Equipment are added to the official defence allocation, Kenya's military expenditure is at least 90 per cent higher than is currently reported. It seems likely that this category is the running cost of the military (since it comes under the heading Economic Analysis, Current Expenditure) and that it is additional money for the military outside the official budget allocation for defence. If it is not additional money, but is a sub-category of the official allocation to defence, then very little is left for other functions, including wages and salaries. As discussed below, these take up close to 80 per cent of the total official defence allocation. If this is the case, and the remaining 10 or 11 per cent of the official defence budget is for development expenditure, then wages and other personal emoluments must be taken care of in some other way—perhaps by the Office of the President under which the DOD comes.

Finally, a recent study of the central government budget in Kenya found that the practice of shifting expenditure from the budget head originally planned to another head is very common.[18] It is difficult to identify which sectors benefit from this practice, but usually it is the government's favoured ministries and departments, such as the Office of the President, where the DOD is located.

---

[17] There have been allegations in the media and by non-governmental research organizations that controversial expenditure was being hidden or presented in the most confusing manner possible, e.g., allegations in 2001 that the Kenyan police bought 4 Russian military aircraft, estimated to be worth about $1 million each, for an inflated price. Moreover, there was no provision in the budget for the purchase of the aircraft. If that could be done for the police, it could be done for the military. Githongo, J., 'Smoke and mirrors: Kenya's magical budget', *The East African*, 25 June 2001; and 'Kenya police buys junk Russian choppers', *The Monitor* (Kampala), 11 June 2001.

[18] Kirira and Mwale (note 5), p. 153.

Table 6.2. The military expenditure of Kenya: recurrent and development expenditure, 1980/81–2000/2001[a]

Figures are in Kenyan shillings and current prices. Figures in italics are percentages.

Fiscal year	Total military expenditure	Recurrent expenditure	Development expenditure	Development as % of total expenditure
1980/81	1 794.8	1 638.6	156.2	*8.7*
1981/82	2 622.8	2 447.4	175.4	*6.7*
1982/83	2 755	2 611	144	*5.2*
1983/84	2 800.6	2 589.8	210.8	*7.5*
1984/85	2 244.4	2 013.4	216.8	*9.6*
1985/86	2 546.8	..	..	..
1986/87	3 335.4	..	..	..
1987/88	4 886.4	..	..	..
1988/89	4 020.2	3 425.9	595.2	*14.8*
1989/90	5 385.2	4 877.8	507.4	*9.4*
1990/91	6 004.2	5 231.5	678.4	*11.3*
1991/92	4 647.6	4 130.5	517.1	*11.1*
1992/93	5 406.2	4 874.2	532.1	*9.8*
1993/94	6 855.8	6 599.6	256.2	*3.7*
1994/95	6 297.2	6 171.5	125.8	*2.0*
1995/96	9 039	8 801.2	237.9	*2.6*
1996/97	10 471.8	10 313.5	158.4	*1.5*
1997/98	10 182.2	10 060.3	122.0	*1.1*
1998/99	10 579.6	10 536.4	43.2	*0.4*
1999/2000	11 427.2	10 346.9	80.4	*0.7*
2000/2001	14 266.1	14 266.1	0.0	*0.0*

[a] All figures are actual expenditure except for 1997/98–2000/2001, which are provisional actual expenditure.

.. = Not available.

Source: Kenyan Ministry of Finance and Planning, *Statistical Abstract* and *Economic Survey* (Kenyan Ministry of Finance and Planning: Nairobi, various years).

IV. The composition of military expenditure

In terms of the breakdown of the budget, personal emoluments (salaries and allowances) take a disproportionate share of the official defence budget. According to all the national sources, especially the *Statistical Abstract* and the *Economic Survey*, recurrent expenditure takes up to approximately 97 per cent of the budget and development expenditure on average about 3 per cent (see table 6.2). Recurrent expenditure is broken down into personal emoluments and O&M, while development expenditure consists of procurement and R&D. Across all these categories, personal emoluments (salaries and allowances) take a disproportionate share of 80 per cent, O&M takes 16 per cent, and the remaining 4 per cent goes to procurement and R&D.[19]

This does not allow for a good maintenance culture, as a much higher percentage is needed for the O&M to keep all equipment in good condition. The ideal percentages, which the armed forces are trying to attain, are: personal emoluments 40 per cent; O&M 30 per cent; and development 30 per cent.[20]

The budget also has a component of 'appropriation in aid', which is basically the income generated by the armed forces themselves. This includes money from: (*a*) participation in UN peacekeeping operations; (*b*) services rendered to the public, such as firefighting; (*c*) the transport of goods for companies and others using air force aircraft; and (*d*) the proceeds of goods disposed of by the force.[21]

V. Trends in and levels of military expenditure

The trend in the official military expenditure of Kenya in the period covered by this study (1981–2002) can be divided into three phases: a fluctuating but generally high phase (1981–90); a declining phase (1991–99); and a rising phase (2000–2002). It was highest in the 1980s, peaking in 1982 when defence accounted for 11.6 per cent of central government expenditure and 4.6 per cent of GDP. The main reason for the increase was the attempted military coup in 1982, which almost shattered the assumption of the apolitical nature of the Kenyan military. In 1987, however, military expenditure rose again, mainly in response to increased sub-regional conflicts, especially in Uganda, where a guerrilla leader (Yoweri Museveni) had just fought his way to power—the first time this had happened in Africa. Even then, the increases were limited to 2.3 and 5 per cent, respectively, and total military expenditure was still less than the 1982 level.

---

[19] Waweru and Osmeru (note 3). See also Macdonald, B. S., *Military Spending in Developing Countries: How Much is Too Much?* (Carleton University Press: Ottawa, 1997), pp. 138–39.

[20] Waweru and Osmeru (note 3).

[21] Waweru and Osmeru (note 3).

The second phase was a period of decline both in level of military expenditure in real terms and in the share of defence in government expenditure. In 1994 military expenditure was at its lowest ever at 37 per cent of the 1982 level in real terms. After this it increased briefly for the next two years but then started to decline again for the rest of the decade. As a share of central government expenditure military expenditure was on average 4.5 per cent—a decline from the average of 9 per cent of government expenditure in the 1980s. The trend in the 1990s is slightly atypical given that this was a turbulent period in terms of domestic politics—a decade of demands by opposition groups for multiparty democracy and government repression of such groups, with a good deal of violence used on both sides. This only strengthens the impression that the trend in Kenya's military expenditure is more externally motivated than is the case in many African states, where internal political tensions have been accompanied by a rise in military spending.

The third phase, which is relatively short, has been characterized by a rising trend in military expenditure. Between 2000 and 2002 it increased by 24 per cent in real terms—a reverse of trend compared with the previous decade. This was the result of a 40 per cent increase in salaries and increases of 75–95 per cent in allowances for all ranks in the military effected from 2000.[22] This rising trend is likely to continue, as another 400 per cent salary increase was granted in July 2003 to all officers in the Kenyan armed forces. The other ranks received a more modest 21 per cent pay increase.[23]

VI. Summary: assessment of data

Data on military expenditure are generally available in Kenya with long historical series. They are also actual expenditure figures. However, there is considerable doubt about their coverage. In particular, the extent to which certain core components of military expenditure, such as military construction and equipment, are included in the official data is not known. While this may not be the result of a deliberate attempt to hide part of military expenditure, the seeming non-inclusion of such a core component of that expenditure

---

[22] 'Soldiers quizzed over pay protest leaflets', *Daily Nation*, 29 July 2003, URL <http://www.nationaudio.com/News/DailyNation/29072003/News/News2907200366.html>.

[23] 'Soldiers quizzed over pay protest leaflets' (note 22).

in the official data would seem to make such data incomplete and, by implication, unreliable and invalid. Why such a considerable portion of the total official defence budget should be missing year after year is difficult to comprehend. However, seen within the context of the often advertised apolitical nature of the Kenyan armed forces, in a continent awash with political armies, perhaps the reason is simply that 'the boys have to be kept happy'.

7. Nigeria

I. Background

In May 1999 Nigeria returned to democracy after 15 years of military rule. Prior to 1984 the country had experienced brief spells of democracy, the first between 1960 (the year of independence) and 1966, and the second between 1979 and 1983. Thus, before 1999 Nigeria had experienced 29 years of military rule in its 39 years of existence as a country. This long experience of military dictatorship left its mark on all aspects of social, economic and political life.

While the legacy of military rule has not been generally pleasant, the level of openness in Nigerian Government and society, evidenced by the number of regular government publications and private and official newspapers, has compared favourably with that of many 'democracies' on the continent. In fact, measured in terms of the amount of publicly available information, the level of openness was almost the same under the military regimes as under the civilian regimes. However, the variant of military leadership which the country experienced in the 1980s was particularly destructive and had a telling impact on its socio-economic and political development. Several institutions, including the civil service which had been the backbone of previous governments, were virtually destroyed, while records were only kept haphazardly. Decrees restricting press freedom were enacted. As a result, virtually all the services providing information on the country became shadows of what they had been as their work slipped down the government's order of priorities. In particular, the annual budget estimate for recurrent and capital expenditure printed by the Federal Ministry of Information, which used to be a mine of data on the country's economic activities, lost some of its value. Some vital data could no longer be included and the annual budget ceased to be readily available to the public. In the light of the generally acknowledged unreliability of national statistics on Nigeria, even while various government data sources were being published regularly, the neglect of such publications could only compound the data problem of the country.

Since military expenditure data are part of the more general national statistics, there can be little doubt that this neglect would also affect them. The fact that vital data on the costs of well-known military operations in which Nigeria was involved in the recent past are missing from the available official documents confirms that lack of proper documentation also affected the country's military expenditure statistics. What is difficult to determine is whether this was just a part of a national problem of poor record keeping, or the result of wilful neglect or deliberate manipulation of statistics in order to hide military expenditure.

II. The available official data

In spite of the long years of military rule, there are several national sources of official military expenditure data. While the regular publication of some data was impeded as military rule became almost a norm, at no time, even under the brutal regime of General Sani Abacha (1993–98), did all the national sources cease to produce official military expenditure data. Although some of these data became more difficult to obtain as the years passed and military rule became entrenched, the existence of a vibrant press and a pool of seasoned military analysts kept the issue of military expenditure in the public domain and the public consciousness, despite military rule and some draconian laws.

There are several sources of primary data on the military expenditure of Nigeria. The main source is the government's *Approved Budget*, which includes military expenditure. Others include the Central Bank of Nigeria's two main publications, its *Annual Report and Statement of Accounts* and its *Statistical Bulletin: Government Finance Statistics*; the *Annual Abstract of Statistics*, published by the Federal Office of Statistics; the annual Appropriation Act; the National Rolling Plan (formerly National Development Plan); the *Report of the Accountant General of the Federation*; and the *Auditor General's Report, Part II*. Each of these is described below.

1. The *Government of the Federal Republic of Nigeria Approved Budget* (henceforth the *Approved Budget*) is the main official publication of the federal government for its annual budget estimates and revenue. Until 1981 it was known as the *Recurrent and Capital Estimate of the Federal Republic of Nigeria*.[1] In 1982 and 1983 the word

---

[1] For an earlier description and analysis of this document see Adekson, J. 'B., Sources and methods for the Nigerian military expenditure data: a research note', *Nigerian Journal of International Affairs*, vol. 10, no. 1 (1981), pp. 89–107.

Revenue was added to the title to reflect the inclusion of expected government revenue from each ministry, including the Ministry of Defence. In 1984 that title was dropped in favour of the current title. The *Approved Budget* was the main source of information for other national sources of data on military spending and of data on other government expenditure until the late 1980s, when its importance diminished as a result of lack of regular updating of figures and of inability to keep pace with the level of government supplementary allocations within the year. Since 2001, it has begun to include some of the details missing from past editions and therefore to regain its importance as the main data source for the government's annual budget estimates.

Military expenditure appears in the *Approved Budget* under the MOD head which, like other budget heads within the document, is divided into: (*a*) revenue, and (*b*) recurrent and capital expenditure. The revenue part records the expected income from the MOD, including profit-yielding defence-related businesses; recurrent expenditure covers items such as personnel and overhead costs; and capital expenditure covers development projects, general operations and maintenance, and the procurement of equipment and training. The *Approved Budget* also contains actual or revised expenditure for the preceding year (until the mid-1980s), and earlier editions of the *Estimates* (the precursor of the *Approved Budget*) contain the actual expenditure for two fiscal years before the current year.

2. The *Annual Report and Statement of Accounts* is the Central Bank of Nigeria's annual report of its activities and statement of its and the federal government's accounts. It summarizes the federal government accounts for the year and gives a functional breakdown of government expenditure for the year by line ministries. Military expenditure is to be found under Defence. As in the *Approved Budget*, it is divided into recurrent and capital expenditure. Unlike the *Approved Budget*, there is no breakdown of either of these categories of expenditure, although this deficiency is compensated for by the fact that it reports data for five years—the current year and the four preceding years. The first three years are usually actual expenditure figures, while the fourth year is a revised figure and the current year a provisional figure.

3. The *Statistical Bulletin: Government Finance Statistics*, also published by the Central Bank of Nigeria, has come out annually since

2001 (before then it was quarterly) and presents government statistics on public finance. Unlike the *Annual Report*, it provides data on the federal government finances from 1977 and regularly adds on the most current year. The data it provides are, however, only estimates and are hardly ever (if at all) improved upon subsequently, even when supplementary allocations are made. Its advantage lies in the long time series. As in the *Annual Report*, military expenditure is to be found under Defence and is divided into recurrent and capital expenditure.

4. The Federal Office of Statistics' *Annual Abstract of Statistics* is a collection of data on the various aspects of the social and economic development of Nigeria. It includes a section on public finance where the breakdown of the federal government's expenditure on different parts of the public sector is given. Here military expenditure data are sometimes provided under the Defence head and sometimes lumped together with other security-related budgets and called Defence and Internal Security or General Administration and Internal Security. When the latter is the case, the traditional breakdown into recurrent and capital expenditure is done under the Defence and Security or the General Administration and Internal Security head, but even when the figure for recurrent military expenditure is given under the Defence head capital expenditure may still be lumped together with General Administration and Internal Security. The only advantage the *Abstract* seems to offer is that it provides data for a five-year period. This does not, however, guarantee that the figures for any of the years will be actual expenditure.

5. The Appropriation Act of the National Assembly is the law by which the legislature authorizes the federal government to spend the money allocated and approved by the legislature. It contains the various allocations to the federal ministries, including the MOD, under which the military expenditure figure is presented. There is also a breakdown into recurrent and capital expenditure. One significant feature of the act which makes it a useful source of military expenditure data for Nigeria is that it includes special funds allocated to specific ministries or institutions for special purposes. Since 1999, the military (and more recently the police) have been regular recipients of this sort of special funding, which is reflected in the act under a separate head (capital supplementation) but not counted as part of the allocation to the MOD. Thus the act gives a bigger picture of how

much really goes into military activities than do other sources, which merely present allocations to line ministries alone and, at best, the aggregate figure for 'capital supplementation'.

6. The National Rolling Plan (formerly National Development Plan), which was introduced in 1990, is the country's medium-term development plan. It includes among others the 'defence and security sector' where planned capital projects of the military and other, paramilitary forces can be found. The annual capital budget estimates of the MOD are supposed to be a pull-out from the Rolling Plan. In fact the Rolling Plan is not usually followed in drawing up the budget, but it is increasingly becoming an important aspect of the defence budget process and therefore useful for an understanding of the strategic programmes of the military. It is also important because it includes the estimated costs of programmes. In some annual budget estimates of the MOD these estimates are reflected in the capital expenditure proposals; in several others they are conveniently ignored.

7. The *Report of the Accountant General of the Federation* and the *Auditor General's Report, Part II* are also good sources of data on military expenditure of Nigeria where they are available. They, especially the former, help in determining actual expenditure as opposed to estimates and also in ascertaining the exact amount of overspending that has occurred over the year and in which part of the budget it occurred. The only problem with them is that they are very difficult to obtain, which makes it near-impossible to compare them with other sources that claim to be publishing actual expenditure data.

The *Government Finance Statistics Yearbook* has reported on Nigeria only once, presumably because the country failed to supply data. This leaves national sources as the most important sources of data on Nigeria's military expenditure.

Comparing the sources

In terms of scope, detail and availability, the *Approved Budget* appears to be the best source of data on military expenditure of Nigeria. Although it lost some of its value from about the mid-1980s, the depth of its coverage and detail is unmatched by any other source of data. It is published annually and until the early 1990s was distributed widely throughout the country. Since then, however, and especially since the late 1990s, it has become difficult to locate anywhere except in the library of the Federal Ministry of Finance, which produces it. Other major libraries rarely have a copy for the public, and buying it is equally difficult as it is not available at the Federal Ministry of Information where the government printing press is situated and the budget is printed.

The data provided by the *Approved Budget* (and the *Estimates* before it) are invaluable, especially in terms of disaggregation of the defence budget into its component parts. No other source has its level of disaggregation. This is why the *Approved Budget* still remains the best source in spite of its weaknesses. The disaggregation of the capital expenditure part of the budget in particular provides useful information on the strategic development plans of the military over the medium term, especially when this is read in conjunction with the Rolling Plan. Similarly, the information provided on the amount of revenue expected by the armed forces from their own activities also goes a long way to provide insights into sources of income to the military other than the budget. Taken together with the Rolling Plan, the *Approved Budget* is a mine of information on military expenditure, and its availability on an annual basis makes it possible to construct a long time series to aid analysis.

However, despite its advantages, the *Approved Budget* has one main drawback. Its figures, especially from the mid-1980s, are estimates. While there is a column in the document for actual expenditure for the preceding year, this is no longer strictly reported every year. Until 1985 actual expenditure figures could be expected to be found in each edition for the previous year, or at least the year before that. This practice ceased in the mid-1980s and instead a revised figure for the preceding year is provided which in fact is usually the same as the estimates. This is in spite of the fact that it became almost the norm from the mid-1980s onwards for successive governments to announce supplementary budgets. By leaving out such allocations in its subsequent editions the *Approved Budget* becomes less representative of the actual level of resources committed to military activities, in spite of its scope, level of detail and availability.

The *Annual Report and Statement of Accounts* of the Central Bank of Nigeria appears to be better than the *Approved Budget* on this score. It publishes actual expenditure figures for at least three of the five years it covers and a revised figure for the fourth year, and, as would be expected, provisional figures for the most current year. It also updates its figures in the subsequent editions and sometimes provides actual expenditure for the year preceding the current year. Usually, it also includes supplementary allocations to various sectors, including defence, made in the course of the previous years. However, this is not always the case. Sometimes the *Annual Report* has omitted the most glaring cases of the military budget being supplemented.

This problem, although it is a major weakness of the *Annual Report*, could be excused as it appears that its definition of what should go under Defence Expenditure is what is allocated to the MOD. In a number of cases, extra expenditure on defence goes under Special Projects or as part of the government's extra-budgetary spending. Since this is usually an aggregate sum, ascertaining the exact amount spent on defence is usually a difficult task. Thus the *Annual Report* remains a credible source of primary data on the actual military expenditure of Nigeria. Its obvious shortcoming is that it is not as detailed as the *Approved Budget* and does not provide any disaggregation beyond the division into the recurrent and capital categories.

The other publication of the Central Bank, the *Statistical Bulletin: Government Finance Statistics*, like the *Approved Budget*, also carries budget estimates but, unlike any of the other sources of primary data, has a long time series, starting in 1977 and continuing to the present, which makes it very useful for time series analysis. However, unlike the *Annual Report* it never updates its figures or adds any supplementary budget for defence in the course of the year to the figure for that year. This reduces its value (as with the *Approved Budget*) since it does not capture total expenditure on military activities. Moreover, its figures are not comparable to those in the *Approved Budget* even though both of them purportedly publish the same estimates. This may be because it never updates its figures. Unlike the estimates of the *Approved Budget*, there is no disaggregation of each category of the budget beyond the broad categorization into recurrent and capital expenditure.

The *Annual Abstract of Statistics* of the Federal Office of Statistics publishes data for five years on various parts of the public sector, including defence. However, its figures are mostly estimates, even though it always claims that the figures for the first three years of the five are actual expenditure and the last two revised estimates and provisional figures, respectively. Of all the sources it is the least reliable.[2] This is partly for the above reason and partly because it is not consistent in its categorization of defence. Sometimes defence stands alone and at other times it is categorized as part of 'internal security'. At other times, especially in the capital expenditure category, it is part of 'general administration'. This lack of consistency in categorization coupled with its publication of estimates as actual expenditure figures makes the *Annual Abstract* of little use as a source of data for military expenditure. It is important that those who are used to finding reliable data on the military expenditure of other African countries in their annual statistical abstracts be wary of the Nigerian version.

The Appropriation Act, as would be expected, contains estimates for the year as approved by the National Assembly and these are broken down into recurrent and capital expenditure. Sometimes the amount requested by the executive is included and the amount approved shown on the side. The significance of the Appropriation Act lies in its presenting the total sum of money requested by government, the purposes for which it was requested, and how much was approved by the National Assembly. It usually reveals military-related expenses not included in the defence budget but declared as 'special projects' of government. No other document does this. This distinguishes the Appropriation Act as a useful complementary source of data on Nigeria's military expenditure.

The National Rolling Plan covers only the capital expenditure parts of the budget but it is particularly helpful when used along with the *Approved Budget*, which contains both recurrent and capital expenditure. Its major drawback is that the projects and the amounts specified for them are not usually included in the annual budget. Until 2000 there were significant variations between the details in the National Rolling Plan and annual capital expenditure.

Both the *Auditor General's Report Part II* and the *Report of the Accountant General of the Federation* are excellent for providing data on actual expenditure and the extent of overspending on defence, but they are difficult to come by and until recently they were not produced regularly (especially the *Auditor General's Report*).

---

[2] For a recent criticism of the Federal Office of Statistics (FOS) figures see Ogidan, A., 'LCCI faults inflation figures from FOS', *The Guardian* (Lagos), 22 July 2003, URL <http://www.guardiannewsngr.com/business/article01>.

III. Data quality

Reliable statistics on different aspects of the socio-economic development of Nigeria are difficult to come by both locally and internationally. Successive governments in the country, which are supposed to be primarily responsible for the compilation of the vital statistics, have never given the task the attention it deserves. Basic national statistics such as those on national population and the number of men under arms are not readily available. Where they are available, they remain contentious. Consequently, a number of international, and even national, organizations requiring statistics about the country in one form or another have had to extrapolate from whatever data can be found. Quite a number of analyses are based on UN, World Bank or IMF statistics.

This is not to suggest that the compilation of statistics on the country does not go on at all. It does so regularly as part of routine government activity, but not with any seriousness, regularity or apparent continuity in the process of compilation or in the data gathered. This calls the reliability of such data into question.

Military expenditure data, as has been seen above, are available from several national sources, especially the government's annual publication of its expected revenue and expenditure for the year in the *Approved Budget*. What is in doubt is their validity—the extent to which the available data on military expenditure represent the totality of the expenses incurred for defence. The problem exists at two levels: (*a*) the lack of comprehensiveness in most national data; and (*b*) the problem of determining actual expenditure on the military as opposed to the estimates approved by the National Assembly for the MOD.

Lack of comprehensiveness

Most of the national sources do not have comprehensive data on Nigeria's military expenditure. There are three reasons for this. The first is the narrow definition of military expenditure as the sums allocated to the Ministry of Defence. The second is the practice of classifying military activities or military-related projects as non-military or as special projects. The third is the lack of regular updating of the available data by the various sources. The three are interlinked.

Perhaps a major reason for the lack of comprehensiveness in the Nigerian military expenditure data is the tendency to regard only the allocation to the MOD as military expenditure. Thus, any other military-related expense that is incurred but that does not pass through the MOD is not counted as part of military expenditure, even though the activity is plainly military. Nigeria's contribution to the Economic Community of West African States (ECOWAS) Monitoring Group (ECOMOG) operation is one such activity. The government regards activities such as peacekeeping or peace enforcement as policy issues and allocates resources for them outside the normal military expenditure,[3] although they are clearly military activities and should be counted as such. Thus, anyone studying Nigeria's military expenditure in the 1990s will be surprised to find that its total official military expenditure between 1990 and 1999 (when it pulled out of ECOMOG)[4] is much less than the estimated $12 billion the country purportedly spent on the operations in Liberia and Sierra Leone during the same period.[5]

Related to this is the practice of classifying activities that are clearly military, or projects that are military-related, as non-military or as special projects which are not counted as part of military expenditure and do not come under the MOD. This is partly responsible for the variation in the figures produced by different sources for the same year, as shown in table 7.1. Military-related projects such as the rehabilitation of military barracks and the payment of military pensions have been designated 'special projects' within the national budget and given special allocations outside the defence budget, and are thus not counted as part of the MOD allocation (and therefore military expenditure). Yet they are clearly military spending. In fact, the construction of military barracks was a major item in the capital expenditure category of the Nigerian defence budget from the mid-1970s to approximately the mid-1980s. Over the six years 1994–99

[3] Omitoogun, W. and Oduntan, T., 'Budgeting for the military sector in Nigeria', Report submitted as part of the SIPRI–African Security Dialogue and Research (ASDR) Project on the Military Budgeting Process in Africa, Mar. 2003.

[4] See the appendix, table A5. Except where otherwise stated, figures on military expenditure, government expenditure and other economic data, and their sources are to be found in the appendix.

[5] 'Obasanjo: leader on a mission for a nation in debt', *Financial Times*, 15 Sep. 2000, p. 6. The exact amount Nigeria spent on ECOMOG operations is still to be properly determined. President Olusegun Obasanjo has estimated it at over $8 billion. Onuora, M. and Oyenka-Ben, T., 'Government takes stock of Ecomog casualties', *The Guardian* (Lagos), 7 July 2002.

Table 7.1. A comparison of data on Nigeria's military expenditure from different national sources, 1993–2002

Figures are in million naira and current prices.[a]

Year	Approved Budget	Central Bank Annual Report	Central Bank Statistical Bulletin	Annual Abstract of Statistics	Ministry of Defence
1993	5 552	. .	4 171	6 382	. .
1994	7 032	. .	5 492	6 609	. .
1995	9 272	. .	7 376	9 360	. .
1996	15 553	. .	14 096	15 686	15 353
1997	17 446	18 286	15 428	18 286	17 446
1998	22 284	25 162	21 279	. .	22 284
1999	37 189	24 567	32 948	. .	30 662
2000	37 692	37 490	40 074	. .	43 687
2001	50 628	63 472	38 066[b]	. .	61 489
2002	59 339	108 148	. .	. .	38 807

. . = Not available.

[a] Figures differ from those provided in the appendix (table A5), because the latter include supplementary allocations that can be reliably identified from other sources.

[b] Recurrent expenditure only.

Sources: Nigeria, *Government of the Federal Republic of Nigeria Approved Budget* (Federal Ministry of Finance, Budget Office: Lagos and Abuja, various issues); Central Bank of Nigeria, *Annual Report and Statement of Accounts* (Central Bank of Nigeria: Abuja, 2001 and 2002); Central Bank of Nigeria, *Statistical Bulletin: Government Finance and Statistics*, vol. 12 (Dec. 2002); *Annual Abstract of Statistics* (Federal Office of Statistics: Abuja, various issues); and Nigerian Ministry of Defence, Budget Office, Abuja, Personal communication.

the Petroleum Trust Fund (PTF), an extra-ministerial agency of the federal government under Sani Abacha, was heavily involved in the rehabilitation and construction of military barracks as well as road building with its own resources outside the official military budget.[6] To exclude from the military budget what used to be a major item of capital investment on the military is effectively to give the military budget another name.

[6] The total income of the PTF from its inception in 1994 to 1999 when it was disbanded was in excess of 181 billion naira (about $1.4 billion). 'How Buhari managed PTF', *The Guardian* (Lagos), 3 Nov. 2002.

In 2002 a supplementary 24 billion naira (about $190 million, or 40 per cent of the 2002 approved budget) in extra money was appropriated for military pensions.[7] Although this was done primarily to compensate for the mismanagement of the military pension scheme in the past—itself a result of the lack of proper record keeping—when it is added to the allocation to the MOD Nigeria's military expenditure rises significantly above the level reported.

From the mid-1980s onwards, supplementary budget allocations became a regular occurrence in the Nigerian budget system. However, most of the national sources of data rarely include the supplementary allocations to defence in their subsequent publications. The *Approved Budget* included them until approximately 1985;[8] the Central Bank of Nigeria's *Annual Report* includes them irregularly. Other sources conveniently ignore such allocations in their subsequent editions, thus making the data incomplete. The only regular source of such data is the local press which publishes them as they are announced and, collectively, is useful in complementing the more reliable sources such as the *Approved Budget* and *Annual Report*.

All this leaves a great deal of military-related expenditure outside the data available on military expenditure in Nigeria.

The problem of determining the actual expenditure of the MOD

The second problem is that of determining the actual expenditure on the military as opposed to the estimates approved by the National Assembly for the Ministry of Defence. While the government publishes how much each ministry is to receive, at the end of the year the actual amount released is not always the same as the estimates approved at the beginning of the year. This is a problem all the national sources of data have to contend with, and it is not peculiar to Nigeria. However, in the absence of a regular report of the Auditor General on the final national accounts for the year, and of an Accountant General's report and financial statement on actual releases and the expenditure of the various ministries, the compilers of the various sources of data prefer to stick to the published estimates and perhaps to the subsequent supplementary allocations.

---

[7] 'Reps pass supplementary appropriation', *The Guardian* (Lagos), 21 Nov. 2002.

[8] In both the 1997 and the 2000 editions of the *Approved Budget*, estimates for the previous year were updated. These were the only exceptions to the general neglect that characterized the data in the *Approved Budget* after approximately 1985.

Table 7.2. A comparison of the Nigerian Ministry of Defence proposed budget, government-announced estimates and actual releases from the government, 1996–2002

Figures are in million naira and current prices.

Year	Proposal (MOD)	Approved estimates	Actual releases (to MOD)
1996	15 353	15 553	15 353
1997	17 446	17 446	17 446
1998	54 545	25 162	22 284
1999	95 094	45 400	30 662
2000	71 202	37 490	43 687
2001	86 617	63 472	75 910
2002	117 848	64 908	38 807

Sources: **Proposals and actual releases**: Nigerian Ministry of Defence, Budget Office, personal communication, May 2003. **Approved estimates 1996 and 1997**: Nigeria, *Government of the Federal Republic of Nigeria Approved Budget* (Federal Ministry of Finance, Budget Office: Lagos and Abuja, 1997 and 1998). **Approved estimates 1998 and 1999 including supplementary allocations as reported in the media, 2000 and 2001**: Central Bank of Nigeria, *Annual Report and Statement of Accounts* (Central Bank of Nigeria: Abuja, 2001 and 2002). **Approved estimates 2002**: Nigerian Senate, Appropriation Act 2002 (National Assembly: Abuja, Mar. 2002).

MOD officials interviewed in the course of this research identified a clear difference between their original budget request to government, the estimate approved by National Assembly as the MOD's annual allocation, and the actual money released by government for their activities which is effectively the budget within which they have to work. There have been serious disagreements between the National Assembly and the executive over the failure of the latter to implement the approved estimates fully.[9] The three amounts vary widely, as table 7.2 shows. Two main reasons account for this variation between proposal, estimates and actual releases. The first is unexpected drops in the level of government revenue, which is highly dependent on oil revenues, but, especially since 1999, the problem has also been associated with the government's intention to cut waste in public sector

---

[9] The problem may reveal a lack of discipline in the budget process. This is examined in the ongoing SIPRI–African Security Dialogue and Research (ASDR) Project on the Military Budgeting Process in Africa. See the SIPRI Internet site at <http://projects.sipri.se/milex/mex_africa_pres.html>.

spending.[10] This has in practice obstructed proper planning. (The MOD's major procurement programme was, however, taken up under other special projects within the wider national budget and this was not reflected in the ministry's annual budget.[11]) The second is the practice already mentioned of making supplementary allocations to various ministries which the different national data sources are hardly able to keep up with.

In table 7.2, columns 1 and 3 are derived from MOD sources. They show that in 2000 and 2001 actual government releases to MOD were greater than the approved estimates. These differences are likely to have been caused by supplementary allocations being made to the MOD after the sources had gone to press, which, since the sources rarely update their data, were not included in the subsequent editions either. In 1999, the amount the MOD claimed had been released to it was 33 per cent below the approved estimate: a supplementary allocation made to defence in that year (shortly after the new civilian government came to power) for the refurbishing of military aircraft may not have passed through the MOD.[12] As a result the MOD never included it as part of its official allocation and expenditure.

In the absence of final government accounts (or an Auditor General's report) all this is difficult to reconcile.

IV. The composition of military expenditure

There is some transparency in the composition of the military budget in Nigeria. Most sources of data have disaggregated data only into recurrent and capital expenditures, but three, the *Approved Budget*, the Rolling Plan and the Appropriation Act, give a further breakdown

[10] Interviews at the Ministry of Defence, Abuja, Nigeria, June 2000 and May 2003. For most of the period when the country was under military rule, the MOD received nearly all of its proposed estimates as budgetary allocation. The only exceptions were in 1998 and 1999 (before the military handed over power to an elected civilian government) when there were regular cutbacks in the approved allocations to other ministries as a result of a drop in expected government revenue (and sometimes when there was no shortfall in revenue). For a recent criticism of this practice by the Chief Justice of the Federation in relation to the budget of the judiciary, see 'National Assembly acted outside the constitution on salary, order of precedence law: Chief Justice Uwais', *Vanguard* (Lagos), 8 Aug. 2003, URL <http://www.vanguardngr.com/articles/2002/features/fe508082003.html>.

[11] Olatuyi, J., 'Govt may go bankrupt by Dec, Kuta warns', *The Guardian* (Lagos), 1 Nov. 2002. Senator Idris Kuta, Chairman of the Senate Committee on Aviation, alleged that the government paid $800 million to Russia for weapons for the armed forces in 2002.

[12] 'How Obasanjo plans to spend N202.2 billion', *The Guardian* (Lagos), 29 July 1999.

Table 7.3. The composition of Nigeria's military expenditure, 1990–2002

Figures are in million naira and current prices.[a]

Year	Recurrent, personnel	Overhead	Capital	Total
1990	1 140	270	818	**2 228**
1991	1 355	479	578	**2 412**
1992	1 456	567	801	**2 824**
1993	2 051	1 034	2 467	**5 552**
1994	3 110	1 095	2 826	**7 031**
1995	3 844	1 500	3 688	**9 032**
1996	8 004	3 621	3 927	**15 552**
1997	7 986	4 516	4 944	**17 446**
1998	8 881	6 254	7 149	**22 284**
1999	25 629	6 903	4 656	**37 188**
2000	23 639	7 108	6 946	**37 693**
2001	24 752	13 309	12 566	**50 627**
2002	38 652	11 756	8 931	**59 339**

[a] The figures for total expenditure differ from those in the appendix (table A.5) because: (*a*) other sources are used for the appendix, and (*b*) known supplementary allocations to the Ministry of Defence and other military-related expenditures are included in table A5.

Source: Nigeria, *Government of the Federal Republic of Nigeria Approved Budget* (Federal Ministry of Finance, Budget Office: Lagos and Abuja, various issues).

of the budget into its component parts. While the Appropriation Act is less detailed, the *Approved Budget* contains a detailed breakdown of different aspects of the budget, including the capital budget.

Recurrent expenditure consists of personnel and overhead costs, which together take 70–90 per cent of the defence budget annually (see table 7.3). Personnel costs take roughly 75 per cent of the recurrent budget, and overhead costs the remaining 25 per cent. Although details of different levels and grades of personnel to be paid are provided in the *Approved Budget*, the number of military personnel is never shown. The expected totals of the salaries for each arm of the services are, however, provided. Capital expenditure usually takes 10–30 per cent of the budget. Recurrent costs, especially personnel costs, are given first charge on the budget.

Capital expenditure consists mainly of what ordinarily should be part of O&M, that is, maintenance of machinery and equipment, construction (mainly of dwellings for military personnel), the renovation and/or maintenance of such buildings, and weapons procurement. Given the assumed size of the Nigerian armed forces (80 000)[13] and the number of military barracks and institutions spread across the country which are supposed to be taken care of by the capital budget, it is not clear how the military can realistically be expected to maintain their equipment or buy new weapons systems. It was no surprise, therefore, that an audit of the armed forces conducted in 1999 found most of their equipment to be faulty and out of order.[14]

V. Trends in and level of military expenditure

Official military expenditure has been declining in Nigeria since 1980 when it constituted 1.6 per cent of GDP. It maintained the downward trend almost throughout the 1980s, increasing only once, in 1983. Two main reasons were responsible for the decline. The first was the general decline in the oil revenue on which the government depended for nearly 90 per cent of its annual income. The second, a corollary to the first, was the depreciation of the currency, the naira, which was at par with the US dollar until approximately 1979 but then started to depreciate from the early 1980s. The increase in 1983 was a result of the general election in that year which resulted in widespread violence in several parts of the country and eventually led to a military coup on 31 December of that year. The civilian president had invested in military equipment and improved salaries for the military in order to nip military intervention in the bud, but this proved abortive. Although in real terms the 1980 level remains the peak to date, military expenditure as a share of central government expenditure and GDP was highest in 1983, at 11.4 per cent and 1.9 per cent, respectively.

In spite of the coup, declining oil revenue ensured that military expenditure resumed its downward slide in 1984. By 1989 it had declined to only 24 per cent of the 1980 level, the lowest level in

[13] Former Chief of Army Staff (1976–79) and Defence Minister (1999–2003) Gen. Theophilous Danjuma put the strength of the Nigerian armed forces at 80 000. Onuorah, M., '"Na" Abba backs downsizing of military', *The Guardian* (Lagos), 16 May 2000; and Oloja, M., Eluemnuor, T. and Onuorah, M., 'Govt drops plan to trim military', *The Guardian* (Lagos), 24 Dec. 2000.

[14] Goldman, A., 'Out of office but still in the picture', *Financial Times*, 3 Mar. 2000.

almost two decades. It also declined both in terms of the share of total government expenditure and as a share of GDP, to 3.1 per cent and 0.6 per cent, respectively, in 1989. In 1990, when Nigeria became involved in the ECOMOG operation in Liberia, military expenditure experienced the first increase in real terms since 1983, of approximately 65 per cent over the 1989 level, but was still only 40 per cent of the all-time peak of 1980. The 1990 increase was sustained the following year with a 50 per cent increase in real terms, but expenditure was still only 61 per cent of the 1980 figure. Military expenditure then fluctuated in real terms and as a share of government expenditure until 1997, when it started a gradual increase again.

Within the period 1991–98, two significant developments with implications for military spending occurred.

One was the presidential election of 1993, which was conducted by the military. The result was judged to be free and fair both locally and internationally, but the military annulled it, much to the chagrin and anger of the people. This caused extensive civil disturbances and violence. Military expenditure in 1993 increased by more than 100 per cent in nominal terms and about 35 per cent in real terms over that of the preceding year. In November 1993 the military again seized power from an interim civilian government installed to resolve the lingering political crisis caused by the annulment of the election results.

The other significant development worthy of note during this period was the currency exchange regime instituted by the military government of Sani Abacha, 1993–98, which essentially favoured the military. While the rest of the country used an exchange rate of 84 naira : $1, the military and some other arms of government (mainly the presidency) enjoyed a special exchange rate of 22 naira : $1, which meant essentially that the declared military expenditure, especially the capital component of the budget, was four times the figure reported.[15]

When Abacha died in 1998 his successor, General Abubakar Abdulsalami, held a general election in 1999 which ushered in a new civilian administration. The new government made a commitment to re-professionalize the armed forces and bring Nigerian troops back from ECOMOG in Sierra Leone. To meet this goal, it requested and got additional money to that year's budgeted military expenditure in

[15] See, e.g., 'Budget '98: the loose ends', *The Guardian* (Lagos), 14 Jan. 1998, p. 14. See also Omitoogun, W., 'Military expenditure in Africa', *SIPRI Yearbook 2000: Armaments, Disarmament and International Security* (Oxford University Press: Oxford, 2000), pp. 291–98.

order to allow it to refurbish the military aircraft which would evacuate the Nigerian troops from Freetown.[16] Thus, total military expenditure for 1999 increased by 87 per cent in real terms over the preceding year, to make up 4.8 per cent of government spending and 1.4 per cent of GDP. This was no doubt a significant increase, but the level of expenditure was still only 73 per cent of the 1980 level in real terms.

The general commitment of the civilian administration to redirect the attention of the armed forces from politics to their traditional role has meant constant provision of additional resources for retraining and modernization of equipment. Thus, since 1999 military expenditure has been rising again, especially as a proportion of central government expenditure. In 2001, for instance, spending was 6.2 per cent of total central government expenditure, a level not seen since 1985.

The overall trend in military expenditure from 1980 is one of general decline and occasional increases almost every 10 years. It has never been as high as 2 per cent of GDP since 1980; the highest-ever was 1.9 per cent, recorded in 1983. Spending in other years has been 1.6 per cent of GDP and below. For most of the 23-year period under review it was below 1 per cent of GDP.

VI. Summary: assessment of data

Data on the military expenditure of Nigeria have always been available in various national sources. However, most of them are not sufficiently comprehensive to reflect the totality of the resources committed to military activities in the country. The problem lies partly in the narrow definition of military expenditure as allocations to the Ministry of Defence and in the government's practice of classifying what are patently military expenditure items under heads other than Ministry of Defence; but it is also partly the inability of the official data sources to keep pace with the government's regular supplementary allocations after the initial annual budget estimates have been announced. There is usually a big difference between the estimates announced and eventual releases to the MOD but, in the absence of an audited account (or official announcement by the MOD itself), the latter are difficult to establish from the various national data sources.

[16] See note 12.

These shortcomings make the various military expenditure data inadequate or not comprehensive enough. While there is no clear evidence of a deliberate attempt by governments to hide military spending, improper classification, including the deliberate classification of military-related projects under budget heads other than Defence, leaves room for suspicion.

Lack of regular audit of the federation's accounts also means that access to the final accounts of the MOD is impossible. It is no surprise therefore that the federal government annual publication on the budget, the *Approved Budget*, ceased to provide actual expenditure figures for past expenditures from the mid-1980s.

This said, the military expenditure of Nigeria can be divided into two periods where reliability is concerned. The first is that from independence in 1960 to 1985, and the second the period since 1986.

Overall, data up to 1985 are more reliable than those for later years. Whichever period one looks at, however, the newspapers of the period should serve as a good supplement to the sources, and especially the more reliable among the latter, the Approved Budget and the Central Bank's *Annual Report and Statement of Accounts*.

8. Uganda

I. Background

For 20 years, from 1966 to 1986, Uganda experienced serious political and economic difficulties occasioned by internal political jostling for power by its diverse ethnic and interest groups. The military played a critical role in, and indeed were central to, the long-drawn-out crisis.[1] It is therefore no surprise that in the post-crisis period the role of the military in the new dispensation and the level of resources committed to maintaining them have received a great deal of attention.[2]

In 1966 Milton Obote, president and prime minister of Uganda, used the army to arrest his opponents and oust the previous president, the Kabaka of Buganda, and introduced a new constitution which placed more power in his own hands. From that time he began to rely on the military as a means of preserving his power.[3] In 1971 Obote was overthrown in a military coup and a colonel in the Ugandan Army, Idi Amin, succeeded him. Amin ruled until 1979, when a combined force of Tanzanian troops and renegade members of the Ugandan National Liberation Army (UNLA) attacked Uganda and forced him to flee into exile. Amin's rule witnessed one of the worst periods in the Ugandan crisis: not only did he destroy all state institutions, including the military, but he also completely ruined the country's economy.

The flight of Amin in 1979 did not bring the expected stability to Uganda. In fact, in the space of two years after he was overthrown, there were three governments in Kampala. The third of these ushered in new elections in December 1980, which were won by former President Obote. In 1985 Obote was again overthrown in another military coup and a new Military Council was set up under General Tito Okello. Meanwhile, as a result of the disaffection caused by the unsatisfactory elections of 1980, a number of groups had initiated

[1] Brett, E. A., 'Neutralising the use of force in Uganda: the role of the military in politics', *Journal of Modern African Studies*, vol. 33, no. 1 (1995), pp. 129–52.

[2] Brett (note 1). See also Colletta, N. and Ball, N., 'War to peace transition in Uganda', *Finance and Development*, vol. 30, no. 3 (June 1993).

[3] Mudoola, D., *Civil–Military Relations: The Case of Uganda*, Occasional Paper no. 5 (Institute of Social Research: Makerere, 1988). See also Mudoola, D., *Religion, Ethnicity and Politics in Uganda* (Fountain Publishers: Kampala, 1993).

guerrilla operations against the government.[4] By late 1985 a former defence minister, Yoweri Museveni, and his guerrilla force, the National Resistance Army (NRA), had entered Kampala and defeated the UNLA. By January 1986 the NRA was effectively in power and calm had returned to most parts of the country, although there were still pockets of resistance in parts of the north. The government needed to pay members of the armed forces, which by then were made up of the remnants of the old army and the members of the NRA, numbering approximately 80 000.[5] To compound the problem, the economy was in ruins and the new government needed to raise money in order to function effectively and meet its obligations both to the people and externally to the country's creditors. Since there was little hope of raising the funds that were needed internally, the attention of the nascent government turned outside the country for support.

II. External assistance

Uganda has always been a recipient of development assistance. It has varied over the years in amount and by type of donor. For instance, between 1962 and the late 1970s the country received only approximately $357 million (or 4 per cent of the total aid it has received since independence),[6] and the bulk of the money came from Russia (between 1962 and 1971) and Libya (after 1974). This situation improved a little from the early 1980s after the return to democracy, when Uganda received on average approximately $143 million annually in aid.[7] In this period the World Bank and other, European bilateral donors began to increase their aid to Uganda.

After 1986, when Museveni and the NRA entered Kampala, the amount of aid received and the number of donors increased dramatically. This was particularly so from 1987 after the new regime accepted the programme of reform proposed by multilateral donors such as the World Bank and the IMF. Aid received increased by almost 35 per cent in 1987 as compared with 1986 and continued to

[4] Amaza, O. O., *Museveni's Long March: From Guerrilla to Statesman* (Fountain Publishers: Kampala, 1998), p. 5.

[5] Colletta and Ball (note 2).

[6] Holmgren, T. *et al.*, 'Uganda', eds S. Devarajan, D. Dollar and T. Holmgren, *Aid and Reform in Africa: Lessons from Ten Case Studies* (World Bank: Washington, DC, 2001), p. 104.

[7] Organisation for Economic Co-operation and Development (OECD) data set available at URL <http://www.oecd.org/dac/stats/>.

grow steadily, reaching an all-time high of \$819 million in 2000.[8] According to data from the Organisation for Economic Co-operation and Development (OECD), aid accounted for over 100 per cent of central government expenditure in 1985 and 1986, and as much as 178 per cent in 1989, only falling to an average of 60 per cent in 1999–2001.[9] Throughout this period the bulk of the assistance was from the multilateral donors—the World Bank and the IMF— followed by European bilateral donors. As Uganda made progress, the donors reviewed their programmes of support and increased support to match various landmark achievements of the new government.

Since Uganda needed all the support it could get in the early stages of the new administration's life, it adapted its national development programme to suit the demands of the donors.[10] Over the years the government's dependence on external sources to fund its major programmes has become a subject of concern and debate: citizens are critical of it as detrimental to the interests of the country. The major concern in this regard is the eagerness with which the government accepts such aid with all the conditions attached, without due consideration for their impact on the population.[11]

The importance of external aid to Uganda indicates great donor influence in the country. Because the new military represented a severe burden on the Museveni Government after 1986, donors, led by the World Bank, supported a programme of demobilization for the army between 1992 and 1996. The programme helped in demobilizing as many as 30 000 of the estimated 80 000 military personnel with full benefits to help them resettle in their local communities. The exercise

---

[8] See the appendix, table A6. Except where otherwise stated, figures on military expenditure, government expenditure and other economic data, and their sources are to be found in the appendix.

[9] See the appendix, table A6. According to other sources, in FY 1992/93, external aid made up approximately 52% of government revenue or 44% of government expenditure, and in 1993/94 the corresponding figures were 42% and 33%. Ugandan Government, *Background to the Budget 1994/1995* and *Background to the Budget 1995/1996* (Ministry of Finance, Planning and Economic Development: Kampala, 1994 and 1995). In FYs 2002/2003 and 2003/2004 donors contributed 52% and 48%, respectively, to the government budget. 'East African budgets', *Africa Research Bulletin*, 16 May–15 June 2003, p. 15655.

[10] Bigsten, A. and Kayizzi-Mugerwa, S., *Crisis, Adjustment and Growth in Uganda: A Study of Adaptation in an African Economy* (Macmillan: Oxford, 1999), p. 5.

[11] Bibala, G., 'Saying no to some donors and investors is wise', *East African*, 23 July 2001.

lasted approximately four years and cost over $40 million.[12] An estimated $13 million administered by the World Bank's International Development Association (IDA) also helped to relieve the pain of retrenchment and the burden on government.[13]

Naturally enough, the government strove to meet the benchmarks set by donors and comply with their conditions even as it struggled to take 'ownership' of the reform process after 1992. One of the conditions believed to have been imposed on the government after the demobilization exercise as the basis for further donor support was that defence expenditure be limited to 2 per cent of GDP.[14]

III. The available official data

Uganda inherited a good civil service structure from the British at independence, and it made the publication of various statistics one of its main tasks. However, by the mid-1970s this had ceased, and many records were either lost or not kept at all. There was also little interest in compiling vital statistics on the country as highly skilled personnel emigrated to neighbouring stable states as well as to Europe and the USA, where there were better career prospects. From the 1980s, therefore, this aspect of the civil service function was one of the main areas which donors helped the government to rebuild.[15] The government

[12] Colletta, N. J., Kostner, M. and Wiederhofer, I., *Case Studies in War-to-Peace Transition: The Demobilization and Reintegration of Ex-Combatants in Ethiopia, Namibia and Uganda* (World Bank: Washington, DC, 1996), p. 309.

[13] Holmgren *et al.* (note 6), p. 132.

[14] There is no publicly available official evidence that this ceiling has been imposed. The Ugandan government generally makes reference to such a ceiling in its annual budget speeches: see, e.g., Ugandan Government, *Budget Speech* (Ministry of Finance, Planning and Economic Development: Kampala, 15 June 2000), p. 19; and Ugandan Government, *Background to the Budget* (Ministry of Finance, Planning and Economic Development: Kampala, 2000), p. 70. Most reports in the press cite a ceiling of 1.9–2 % of GDP as the limit imposed by donors. The strongest indication yet that a specific ceiling is imposed by donors was given in a letter written by President Museveni to Clare Short, then British Secretary of State for International Development, in Aug. 2001 asking for the support of the British government to convince other donors to allow Uganda to increase its military expenditure. Mwakisyala, J., Ngotezi, A. and Wakabi, W., 'UK moves to prevent Uganda, Rwanda clash', *The East African*, 22 Oct. 2001, URL <http://www.nationaudio.com/News/EastAfrican/29102001/Regional/Regional19.html>. In 2002 the donors, led by the United Nations Development Programme (UNDP) and the USA, supported Uganda's request to be allowed to increase its military expenditure. 'Uganda: new US ambassador supports boosting defence budget to tackle terrorism', *New Vision* (Internet edn), 14 Nov. 2002, in Foreign Broadcast Information Service, *Daily Report–Africa* (FBIS-AFR), FBIS-AFR-2002-1114, 15 Nov. 2002.

[15] Bigsten and Kayizzi-Mugerwa (note 10), p. 31.

itself paid renewed attention to the compilation and dissemination of statistics. As part of the adjustment efforts strong emphasis was put on the rehabilitation of data-gathering units, especially the Statistics Department of the Ministry of Finance, Planning and Economic Development.[16] The new Ugandan Bureau of Statistics (UBOS) was created in 1998 out of the Statistics Department as a result of these efforts.[17]

There were thus fresh efforts to make a new beginning by reconstructing the past, especially where records had been lost. Beginning from the early 1980s, and especially from the mid-1980s under President Museveni, data on various aspects of the socio-economic life of Uganda started to appear again regularly and with regular improvement in terms of the detail provided.

Military expenditure has been a part of the statistics, being an important aspect of government expenditure and one in which the donors of development assistance showed great interest. However, in spite of the new government interest in gathering and publishing data about the country, there was little public awareness of their existence because of lack of publicity and lack of access to the published data. Again, it would appear that in the early period (1985–93) the data were published more as part of the effort to satisfy donors, who insisted on their regular compilation and publication, than as part of an effort to inform the general public. This can be deduced from the limited numbers of copies of the publications made available and the difficulty of obtaining them.[18] It was not until around 1999, again through donor insistence, that deliberate efforts began to make the general public aware of the publications and in particular the process of drawing up the budget.[19] The cost of buying the publications is also prohibitive, by local standards, making them inaccessible to the ordinary people.

---

[16] Bigsten and Kayizzi-Mugerwa (note 10), p. 31.

[17] On the history of its founding see the UBOS Internet site at URL <http://www.ubos.org/hindex1.html>.

[18] Although the author was able to get copies of the publications he needed—budget speeches and the *Background to the Budget* (various issues)—it took the assistance of an official at the Ministry of Finance, Planning and Economic Development to get some back copies, and especially the more recent editions, which were finally obtained from the office of a senior official in the ministry.

[19] See, e.g., the budget speech 2002 for the government's admission of the need to make the public aware and involve it in its various programmes at the planning stage. Ugandan Government, *Budget Speech* (Ministry of Finance, Planning and Economic Development: Kampala, 15 June 2002), p. 28.

Two main types of primary source on the military expenditure of Uganda are identifiable—national and international. There are three national sources—the *Background to the Budget*, the *Budget Speech* and the *Statistical Abstract*. The two former are published by the Ministry of Finance, Planning and Economic Development and the *Statistical Abstract* by the UBOS, a semi-autonomous body that was part of the same ministry up to 1998.

1. The *Background to the Budget* is published every year prior to the budget but in the same month (June) as the budget is read to Parliament by the finance minister. Its main aim is to provide insight into the budget and the policies that informed it. It highlights the major developments in the performance of the economy in the previous year and the first half of the current year. It also brings into focus actual government expenditure for the previous six fiscal years and, as from FY 1995/96, includes an extensive outline of the government's medium-term expenditure plans and strategy. The document contains defence expenditure in the recurrent and capital expenditure categories, and gives the percentage of overall government expenditure each accounts for. In the medium-term expenditure category it gives a breakdown of the recurrent expenditure of the defence budget.

2. The *Budget Speech* is the annual government statement of economic and fiscal policy for the new fiscal year. It usually contains the preliminary government expenditure out-turn for the year just ending and the estimates for the next fiscal year, with the traditional breakdown into recurrent and capital expenditure. Since the mid-1990s it has also contained the government's Medium-Term Expenditure Framework (MTEF) for the next three years.

3. The annual *Statistical Abstract* contains data on different aspects of the socio-economic development of Uganda. It publishes data on military expenditure as part of its section on Public Finance. Usually it publishes figures for five years including the current fiscal year. All figures for the previous four fiscal years are actual expenditure. The last in the series is, as might be expected, approved estimates. The *Statistical Abstract* also provides the share of defence in the totals for each category of expenditure (recurrent and development).

The only international source of data on the military expenditure of Uganda is the *Government Finance Statistics Yearbook*.[20]

[20] On the *Government Finance Statistics Yearbook* see chapter 1, section I.

Comparing the sources

On the whole the national sources seem to agree in various respects, especially on the recurrent figures, perhaps as a result of being from the same source (the Ministry of Finance, Planning and Economic Development) until 1998. The *Background to the Budget* appears to be the best in terms of the information provided. Moreover, most of its figures are also actual expenditure and span a minimum of six years. This is in addition to the information on the MTEF from the mid-1990s. It also indicates that expenditure on the paramilitary group known as the Local Defence Units (LDUs) is not included in the defence budget in the MTEF section. However, valuable as the *Background to the Budget* is as a source of data on the military expenditure of Uganda, it does not provide enough detailed information on its components beyond the recurrent/capital expenditure breakdown.

Beyond this it provides no other information that can help an understanding of Uganda's military expenditure. Instead, it tends to confuse to the extent that its later issues often contradict the figures given in earlier editions. For instance, actual recurrent expenditure for defence for FY 1994/95 was given as 9.1 billion shillings in the 1995/96 edition and 111.7 billion shillings in the 2000/2001 edition. Moreover, it is not consistent in giving the government's capital expenditure figures. Earlier editions contained actual capital defence expenditure, but the 2000/2001 edition did not include them. This makes comparing earlier and later figures difficult. It also makes the construction of a long and consistent time series problematic. All the same, the *Background to the Budget* is a good source of information on the defence expenditure of Uganda once the user is aware of these shortcomings.

The *Budget Speech* has figures for only two years—expenditure for the outgoing fiscal year and estimates for the incoming fiscal year, neither of which is actual expenditure, so that its value is limited. Thus, it is useful only as a complement to the *Background to the Budget*, which does not usually include figures for the incoming year, and for indicating the policy thrust of government for the coming year.

The *Statistical Abstract* gives military expenditure data for five years, usually including the current fiscal year. It provides approved estimates for the year before the current fiscal year, as would be expected, and actual expenditure figures for the three years preceding that. Like the *Background to the Budget*, it also breaks down the data into recurrent and capital expenditure, and provides the percentage each constitutes of total government recurrent and capital expenditure. Unlike the *Background to the Budget* it provides an economic and functional classification of capital development expenditure, which gives an insight, however slight, into the breakdown of the development expenditure for defence. This breakdown is limited to the most current year in the series, but it is not to be found in any other publication. In this regard the *Statistical Abstract* is a step ahead of the other sources and seems to live up to its aim of being a 'convenient volume for statistical reference and a guide to other statistical publications and sources' with timely and reliable statistics.[21]

IV. Data quality

The question how reliable the official military expenditure data of Uganda are should be viewed within the context of the country's political economy. Uganda is torn between the need to satisfy the donors, who contribute substantial parts of its government expenditure, and the need to provide for its security with resources it deems adequate. After the donors helped to fund the demobilization of a considerable proportion of the armed forces between 1992 and 1996, as mentioned above, they stipulated that military expenditure should not exceed 2 per cent of GDP annually.

This ceiling has been a major problem for the Ugandan government, which feels that it has the right to provide adequately for the country's security. The government has argued that the ceiling is not realistic in view of the security threat posed by the rebel activities in the north and west of the country. In 2001 Museveni openly asked the donors to lift the ceiling to enable Uganda to spend more on security so that it could protect itself properly from its neighbours and the rebel forces. In doing so he asked for twice what the country had spent in 2001 for the coming three years[22]—a level he clearly regarded as realistic for Uganda's security. While the donors did not allow Uganda to make such an increase until 2002, it is believed that in one way or another it had been getting its way in any case, as it used its powers over the

---

[21] Ugandan Bureau of Statistics, 'Foreword' [to the *Statistical Abstract 2001*], URL <http://www.ubos.org/abstractpdf/forward.pdf>.

[22] 'UK moves to prevent Uganda, Rwanda clash' (note 14).

implementation of the budget to initiate discretionary spending which usually favoured defence. Many saw this request to donors as merely an attempt to allow what was already being done discreetly to be done openly and officially.[23]

Uganda practises a cash budgeting system which allows only revenue that is generated to be spent. The Ministry of Finance, Planning and Economic Development has the power to distribute the money to line ministries as cash is collected and according to need. Usually defence is favoured, and frequently other ministries do not get the whole of the money budgeted for them while the Ministry of Defence gets more than it was officially allocated.[24] How much it gets in addition to its official allocation in the budget is known only to the officials at the Ministry of Finance who allocate the resources. Some revelations about the disbursement of funds to the line ministries would seem to support this conclusion.

The Auditor-General of Uganda in his 2001 annual report to Parliament reported that nearly 8 billion shillings (almost the equivalent of the budgeted development expenditure for 2000/2001, and more than the 1999/2000 development expenditure for defence) had been transferred to the Ugandan People's Defence Forces (UPDF) from the Ministry of Internal Affairs and Police Headquarters to cater for various operations and salaries of units of the UPDF.[25] This was in addition to other unauthorized expenditures that were pointed out in the report to Parliament, amounting to over 3 billion shillings. This confirms the use of resources from other sectors to fund the military. Earlier, during an inquiry into corruption in the Uganda Police Force in 1999, it was stated that the government deliberately allocated exceptionally large amounts to the police and then asked the police to transfer this fund to the UPDF, where the excess was originally intended to go.[26] The essence of the practice was to avoid the prying eyes of the donors who insisted on the 2 per cent ceiling for military expenditure.[27]

[23] Interview with Dr Nkuuhe Johnson, Member of Parliament, Kampala, June 2000.

[24] Johnson (note 23).

[25] Ugandan Auditor General, *Report of the Auditor General to Parliament on the Public Accounts of the Republic of Uganda for the Year Ending 30th of June 2001, Vol. 1* (Office of the Auditor General: Kampala, June 2001), p. 155.

[26] 'Creative accounting in Africa: hidden skills', *The Economist*, 9 Oct. 1999, p. 64.

[27] It is convenient to argue that the imposed spending limit is constraining the government's ability to defend the country effectively, but there is little evidence to suggest that the existing level of spending is being used judiciously. The local press has been full of stories of

Furthermore, other sources of income for the armed forces, such as their factory that manufactures small arms and light weapons, are not accounted for in the military budget. Ideally, this revenue should go to the Treasury, but in most cases much of it is retained for use by the military.[28] The Ugandan Army train the paramilitary LDUs but their funding comes under the Ministry of Internal Affairs (in contrast to the situation in many francophone countries, in which the paramilitary gendarmerie receive the same training as the army and their funding comes under the Ministry of Defence). This allows for funds to be transferred to the MOD from Internal Affairs for the training and other services rendered to the LDUs.

All this points to the fact that the military expenditure figures for Uganda may not be totally reliable and could be no more than a rough indication of what the country is spending on its armed forces.

At the domestic level there is a general belief that the level of military expenditure is justified if it provides adequate security. The government regularly indicates in the budget speech that security is its first priority because, in President Museveni's words, 'Without a state, you cannot have economic development, security is fundamental for the development of the country'. Uganda thus aims to preserve its territorial integrity before any other goal. Internally there is a corresponding degree of understanding of the reasons for high military expenditure, even though many began to query this when the country entered the war in the DRC.[29]

V. The composition of military expenditure

Table 8.2 shows the military expenditure of Uganda broken down into recurrent and development expenditure. The former consists of wage

imports of weapons that were neither of good quality nor a good bargain for the country. One such story concerned the purchase by the government in 1997 of military helicopters from Belarus. They were not in good condition and the unit price was alleged to have been inflated. Pressure on the government from the press and donors for an investigation led to the establishment of a commission of inquiry in 2001. Its report was only released in May 2003, over a year after the report was handed to the government. It is believed that it was released as a result of pressure from the donors. 'Probe reports must lead to jailing culprits', *The Monitor* (Kampala), 19 May 2003.

[28] Interview with Majors Lawnena Kiths and Gerald Maswere, and with MPs, Kampala, June 2000. The MPs noted that this is a common practice with all government income-generating agencies and is intended to encourage them to be more productive. The problem is that no one is sure how much is retained and how much goes to the Treasury.

[29] Interviews with MPs and staff at Makerere University, Kampala, June 2000.

and non-wage parts, while development expenditure consists of several elements, including a strategic element (arms acquisition), procurement (other goods), transport, communications, and construction. The non-wage part of recurrent expenditure consists of running costs (O&M) and others such as training, which is given great emphasis in the UPDF.[30] As in many other African states, recurrent expenditure takes a disproportionate share of total military expenditure—on average roughly 86 per cent annually. The highest share which development expenditure received in Uganda over the two decades covered by this study was approximately 27 per cent, in 1990, and the lowest was in 1992 when it received just 2 per cent of the total military allocation.

VI. Trends in and levels of military expenditure

The level and trend of Uganda's military expenditure have been determined by three factors: (a) the political crises and war the country has experienced since 1966, (b) the influence of donors of development assistance, and (c) external (sub-regional) security factors.

In the 1980s, military expenditure constituted a huge burden on the Ugandan government at an average of more than 23 per cent of total expenditure.[31] In 1988 it was approximately 26 per cent of central government expenditure. By 1990, in real terms it was 17 per cent higher than the previous year and as a share of GDP had increased from 2.5 per cent in 1989 to 3 per cent (although as a share of government spending it fell between 1989 and 1990 as a result of the huge external budgetary support which the government received from donors of economic aid).

The unsustainably high level of spending on defence was caused by the large number of military personnel the new government had to maintain. On capturing power after years as a guerrilla movement, it decided to integrate the remnants of the Ugandan Army into the victorious guerrilla army of the NRA to form a new UPDF. The result was a large army of approximately 80 000 men which could only be maintained at the expense of other sectors of the public service. As already mentioned, donors, especially the World Bank, helped in the demobilization of some of the UPDF personnel after 1992.

---

[30] Interview with Majors Kiths and Maswere, Bombo Barracks, Kampala, June 2000.
[31] See the appendix, table A6.

Table 8.1. The military expenditure of Uganda: recurrent and development expenditure and their respective shares of total central government expenditure, 1982/83–1999/2000

Figures are in million Ugandan shillings and current prices. Figures in italics are percentages.

Fiscal year	Recurrent military exp. A	Recurrent military exp. as % of central govt exp. B	Military exp. on development C	Military development exp. as % of central govt exp. D	Total (A + C) E
1982/83	67.9	*15.47*	23.3	*26.42*	91.2
1983/84	166.5	*27.61*	25.8	*15.66*	192.3
1984/85	356.3	*20.12*	28.5	*7.53*	384.8
1985/86	1 026.9	*24.84*	33.2	*4.68*	1 060.1
1986/87	2 212.4	*27.56*	400.1	*17.88*	2 612.5
1987/88	6 383.1	*23.46*	2 229	*23.82*	8 612.1
1988/89	16 781.4	*28.76*	3 800	*31.48*	20 581.4
1989/90	34 697	*33.61*	4 242	*17.75*	38 939
1990/91	40 320	*32.96*	16 593	*31.87*	56 913
1991/92	52 410	*18.5*	3 737	*10.6*	56 147
1992/93	58 664	*15.6*	1 025	*3.2*	59 689
1993/94	75 576	*22.8*	4 332	*7.2*	79 908
1994/95	111 607	*20.1*	..	..	111 607
1995/96	124 343	*23.3*	..	..	124 343
1996/97	147 618	*27.1*	5 180	*4.32*	152 798
1997/98	138 214	*21.1*	11 399	*7.90*	149 613
1998/99	226 542	*24.4*	7 628	*3.59*	234 170
1999/2000	223 029	*25.9*	7 487	*2.6*	230 516

Note: The Ugandan fiscal year runs from April to March. The figures in this table are therefore not directly comparable to those in the appendix (table A6), which are adjusted to the calendar year.

.. = Not available.

Sources: Ugandan Ministry of Finance, Planning and Economic Development, *Background to the Budget 1989/90, 1992/93, 1995/96 and 2000/2001* (Ministry of Finance, Planning and Economic Development: Kampala, 1989, 1992, 1995 and 2000); and Ugandan Bureau of Statistics, *Statistical Abstract 2001* (Ugandan Bureau of Statistics: Kampala, 2002).

By 1993, when the donor-supported demobilization exercise had started, defence spending went down sharply to approximately 9 per cent of central government expenditure, and in real terms was about 70 per cent of the level of 1990.

However, no sooner was demobilization under way than new insurgencies started, first in the north of the country and then in the west, which necessitated another round of resource mobilization to ward off the insurgents. This naturally resulted in another round of increases starting in 1993. Since 1993 military expenditure has maintained a steady rise in real terms, reaching a peak in 2002 when it was 69 per cent higher than the 1990 level. As a share of central government expenditure, however, military expenditure has stayed below the 23 per cent average of the 1980s and in 2001 was just over 9 per cent.

As a share of GDP, military expenditure has also declined from the average of 2.6 per cent in the 1980s to 2.1 per cent in the 1990s. This has been attributed to the donors' insistence on a maximum spending level of 2 per cent of GDP. In 1998 and 1999, when the government exceeded this limit, donors, led by the multilateral agencies, and especially the IMF, suspended aid to Uganda and only resumed lending when the government reverted to the imposed limit.[32] In 2002, the government again overshot the limit, but this time with the support of the donors, to enable it to equip itself for the war against the insurgent group, the Lord's Resistance Army (LRA) in the north of the country.[33] Uganda's involvement in the war in the neighbouring DRC, the unease in relations with its former ally, Rwanda, and the internal insurgent movements in the north and west of the country have been some of the reasons for the steady rise in military spending over the past decade, particularly from 1998.

VII. Summary: assessment of data

Data on several aspects of the socio-economic development of Uganda are becoming readily available. Military expenditure data are available as part of this new process of compiling and disseminating vital statistics on the country. In this new effort, the donors of development assistance to Uganda have been crucial, especially in

[32] Mwenda, M. A., 'Domestic debt record shs 100 bn, IMF suspends aid to Uganda', *The Monitor* (Kampala), 13 Mar. 1999.
[33] 'Uganda: new US ambassador supports boosting defence budget to tackle terrorism' (note 14).

providing technical and financial support and often initiating new programmes.

Security is one of the key areas where donors have supported and remain interested in Uganda. This has had the advantage of making data on this critical aspect of the public sector available, including for earlier years. However, donor insistence on a maximum level of spending on defence which the government has consistently argued is below the level needed to guarantee national security creates room for doubt as to whether the government can actually have been keeping faith with the donors on the imposed spending ceiling. The discovery of overspending on defence in 1998 and 1999, the allegation that funds were moved from the police to the army, and the request to the donors for increased spending on defence in 2001 all point to a possible failure to adhere to the spending limit. Yet the government has consistently provided data suggesting that military expenditure has been at the level expected.

Again, the long years of war in Uganda are likely to have made the historical series unreliable as well. It is almost impossible to capture all expenditure on military activities in wartime, especially in an underdeveloped economy such as Uganda's. Data on the war years, especially 1979–86, can be taken only as a broad indication of what was spent. Similarly, the Ugandan government's involvement in the DRC war and the allegation that individuals within the UPDF have been involved in stripping the DRC of its mineral wealth make the data unreliable. In addition, some of the UPDF's additional income does not go into the budget for the military, so that the available expenditure data do not fully reflect total expenditure on military activities.

There may be a difference after 2002, when the donor-imposed ceiling was lifted to allow Uganda to spend at an increased level and support its war against the insurgents in the north of the country. The 15 per cent increase in real terms in 2002 over spending in 2001 may be a reflection of the extent of overspending in the preceding years, when fear that the donors might suspend aid prevented Uganda from openly admitting its actual expenditure on defence.

9. Conclusions: towards a better understanding of military expenditure in Africa

I. Introduction

From the preceding chapters some general conclusions can be drawn about military expenditure data for African states.

1. Contrary to the general perception, data are indeed available in the African countries examined in this study. However, there is a general lack of detail in the military expenditure data provided by states, which makes thorough analysis difficult, if not impossible.

2. The availability of data varies from country to country. Similarly, the reasons why data are available differ from country to country, and such reasons often impact significantly on the reliability and validity of the data.

3. The quality of the available data also varies from country to country and even between sources within the same country. There is a general lack of consistency in the coverage of the defence budget over time and often uncertainty as to what is covered, which creates doubts about the reliability of the data.

4. In a few cases where the data are relatively reliable, there are doubts as to their validity—the extent to which the data represent the total expenses on the armed forces. Off-budget spending on defence seems to be a common feature in all the countries studied.

5. The lack of reliable and valid data in these countries (and possibly other African countries) has implications for the analysis of trends and levels of military expenditure.

6. The problem of data quality and the particular characteristics of the military expenditure of each of the different countries studied here make it more difficult to identify and understand the determinants of military expenditure in these countries (and Africa as a whole). As a result it is difficult, if not impossible, to make generalizations about the determinants of military expenditure for all of Africa.

This concluding chapter discusses the findings of this study in relation to the availability and quality of data, and their implications for the analysis of trends and levels of military expenditure in the six countries. It also recommends measures that could help to improve data availability in the region.

II. The availability of data

Data on military expenditure are published annually in all the countries examined. The most common publications are the annual budget estimates (the national budgets) and statistical yearbooks, and in nearly all the countries covered by this study these are of greater value than other sources, such as the annual reports of central banks, parliamentary reports and debates, and government gazettes. Their availability and usefulness vary between the countries.

Both budget estimates and statistical yearbooks have long historical time series, although they are difficult to locate in some countries, largely because of poor record-keeping and the fact that very few copies are published. Even the government offices responsible for publishing them seldom keep copies a few years after publication. Moreover, although they are supposed to be available for sale, they are often out of stock or too expensive, especially for the private citizen, so that very few people or even organizations have access to them. The distribution of the annual budget estimate, which is the more popular of the two types of publication in all the countries examined here, is restricted; in many instances, only government ministries and a few interested individuals and agencies have access to it. The government gives publicity to selected aspects of the budget, which may or may not include defence, through the local media.

The statistical yearbooks in most of the countries contain actual expenditure figures which make them very useful for analysis. However, their distribution is even more limited than that of the annual budget estimate and they are less well known as a source, and thus hardly used by those looking for military expenditure data. They are published for planning purposes and for sale to those interested in the different data. Over the years, as a result of lack of custom and reduced government funding, the number of copies printed in some countries has been even further reduced.

The establishment of democracy in nearly all the African countries has opened up other sources of information, such as the proceedings of parliaments, especially for the annual budget estimate and sometimes for actual expenditure figures. In a few cases, access to parliamentary debates on the content and composition of the defence budgets is now possible, giving better insight to military expenditure data.

The availability of data differs between countries, but the factors affecting it can be summarized under two headings that apply to all of them: (*a*) the diminished capacities of countries to compile statistics; and (*b*) the demand for data, including military expenditure.

Diminished state capacity to compile data

The institutional capacity to produce the annual budget document has diminished over the years in many African countries,[1] including those examined here. In the past the civil service was the main employer and the first direct source of employment for new graduates, but in many cases the downsizing of the public sector and low wages have led to a mass exodus of highly qualified personnel to the private sector and aid agencies, where salaries are commensurate with their professional qualifications.[2] Others, especially those who trained abroad, have found better jobs outside their countries. The agencies hardest hit by the exodus include the ministries of health, education and finance, central banks and offices of statistics across the continent.

As a general rule, from the immediate post-independence years until the late 1980s the national civil services had the most qualified personnel to carry out high-level tasks, including budget preparation and the compilation of statistics, but a massive loss of manpower during the era of structural adjustment after the mid-1980s reduced countries' capacity to perform these functions. In some countries, budgets are sometimes announced only in the middle of the financial year.[3] In others, when government agencies are 'pressed for time', they merely replicate the previous year's figures or add a certain percentage to the previous year's budget for all ministries 'to allow for inflation' (this is generally known as 'incremental budgeting'). In such circumstances only a few copies of the new budget are made for the ministries or in

---

[1] Bräutigam, D. L., *Aid Dependence and Governance* (Almqvist & Wiksell International: Stockholm, 2000), pp. 38–48.

[2] Lindauer, D. L., Meesook, O. A. and Suebsaeng, P., 'Government wage policy in Africa: some findings and policy issues', *World Bank Research Observer*, vol. 3, no. 11 (1998).

[3] Bräutigam (note 1), p. 44. Nigeria was notorious for this during the era of Gen. Sani Abacha, 1993–98.

some cases only the presidency has copies. In others the budget may never be printed.

This is also one reason for the difficulties many of these countries face in responding to questionnaires on their military expenditure sent out by reporting institutions, such as SIPRI, and international organizations, such as the UN and even the IMF statistical office. The capacity to comprehend the details of the questionnaires is lacking and they are simply not dealt with. In other cases, red tape is the main reason for the lack of response. In the absence of a proper channel of communication between the relevant government ministries (finance, defence and information), it is difficult to complete a standardized questionnaire on military expenditure. In many instances, none of these ministries expressly accepts responsibility for making such information available, preferring to ask for permission from a higher authority, and in the absence of a policy on such issues the higher authority does not respond to the request for permission and the questionnaire is filed away or 'kept in view'.

Realizing the depth of the problem, some donors, notably the World Bank but also bilateral donors, are sponsoring capacity-building projects across Africa in the area of statistics.[4]

The demand factor

The demand for data has a fairly strong impact on their availability. Three sources of demand for military expenditure data can be identified. These are: (*a*) the donors of economic aid, (*b*) the local research community working on security issues, and (*c*) the local media. Singly or collectively, these sources of demand play a role in making data on military expenditure available to the general public.

Donors. The donor community is a strong and influential source of demand. It appears that data are generally more readily available in many aid-dependent countries than in others where a donor presence is minimal or negligible. Of the countries covered by this study, data are available on all aspects of social and economic life in all except Nigeria, where the donor presence is negligible. Indeed, in many East and Southern African countries, where external assistance accounts for 25–60 per cent of governments' budgets and where major devel-

---

[4] World Bank, 'Capacity building in statistics: statistical capacity and development. Concepts and approaches', URL <http://www4.worldbank.org/afr/stats/cap.cfm>.

opment projects are donor-sponsored, the level of data availability, including military expenditure data, is high.

Donors demand transparency and accountability in financial matters from the recipients of aid. They therefore insist on a very detailed budget breakdown and proper dissemination of the budget document in many of the countries in which they play a significant role. Since the late 1980s emphasis has been placed on making military expenditure data available as well, given the burden such expenditure places on the limited resources of many of the countries. That is why, in countries where their support is significant, donors have often made resources for data-generating departments a special focus of their support. This is the case in Cameroon, Kenya and Uganda. Ghana, too, has been receiving similar support recently.

Thus, donors' demand for transparency and accountability in the budgeting process is a major factor in data availability. In order to satisfy the demands of their financiers, countries prepare elaborate budget breakdowns with sections for actual expenditure for the previous years.

Comparing the situation in the countries mentioned above with that in Nigeria, there is a sharp contrast. Data are lacking for several key aspects of the country, including even its total population. Figures for the latter have been a subject of much controversy. The donor presence in the country is negligible, while the years of military rule have been an obstacle to accountability.

With the exception of some smaller states, countries in the other regions of Africa are less dependent on external support than those in East and Southern Africa, and this limited donor presence restricts donor influence in the budget process. It is no surprise that West and Central Africa are the two most difficult regions in terms of data availability in Sub-Saharan Africa.

The local research community. The presence of a sizeable local research community interested in military-related information is a factor in the availability of data on defence. This can be seen in Nigeria and South Africa, where there are large groups of researchers interested in security studies generally and military affairs specifically. The Nigerian case is particularly illustrative. Military rule encountered intense academic and media opposition. Central to the criticisms was the lack of accountability in public expenditure and 'excessive' spending on defence by the military because of their privileged position in power. To disprove this, the military and their political advisers engaged in open debate with the academic community.[5] In the late 1980s, for example, former leader General Ibrahim Babangida and his military aides engaged part of the Nigerian academic community in a series of debates on the level of military expenditure.[6] The debate was so intense and lively that it drew broad public attention to the level of resources devoted to the military.

While the academics pointed out that defence received the highest share of government expenditure annually, or at worst the second-highest, at the expense of education and health, the military maintained that they were not given any undue advantage. The reason why defence received one of the largest allocations in the budget was that it is funded only by the federal government, while every other sector is funded at both federal and state level. If the funding of other sectors at the state level were added to their funding at the federal level, then the funding of all other sectors would exceed that of defence by a wide margin. In order to support the position of the military and show that the military sector was not unduly favoured, reference was always made to the published data on military expenditure and other aspects of social and economic sectors of the country.[7]

The situation in East Africa is markedly different. Except in Kenya, there are few academics in the strategic studies field, so that demand for military expenditure data from the academic community is neg-

---

[5] That is, those who were not detained on the grounds that they posed a threat to state security.

[6] The debate was sparked by an article on Nigeria's military and social expenditure written by the Nigerian scholar J. 'Bayo Adekson (now J. 'Bayo Adekanye). Adekson, J. 'B., 'On the theory of modernizing soldiers: a critique', *Current Research on Peace and Violence*, vol. 8, no. 1 (1978). He followed up the article with a book on Nigerian civil–military relations in which the issue of military versus social and expenditure was further discussed. Adekson, B., *Nigeria in Search of a Stable Civil–Military System* (Westview Press: Boulder, Colo., 1981), pp. 51–71. A senior member army officer, Maj.-Gen. I. B. M. Haruna, replied to the issues raised by Adekson in Haruna, I. B. M., 'Nigerian military and social expenditure 1970–76', *New Nigeria*, 18 May 1982. In Mar. 1985 Maj.-Gen. Ibrahim Babangida, Nigeria's Army Chief of Staff (who became head of state 6 months later through a military coup) picked up where Haruna had left off by criticizing Adekson's position on overspending on defence. Babangida, I. B., 'Nigeria's defence policy within the framework of national planning', Gold Medal on Public Affairs Series, 1 Mar. 1985, published in *The Valiant: Journal of the Nigerian Defence Academy*, vol. 14 (Jan./June 1986). A broad debate ensued, reflected in the number of articles on the subject in the media by academics, journalists and military personnel after Mar. 1985. For a comprehensive list see Dada, A. S., 'Nigerian defence and security: a select bibliography', in A. E. Ekoko and M. A. Vogt, *Nigerian Defence Policy: Issues and Problems* (Malthouse Press Ltd: Lagos, 1990), pp. 332–46, and especially the sections on 'Nigerian defence and development' and 'defence budgeting', pp. 336–39.

[7] Haruna (note 6).

ligible, if not non-existent. Similarly, among the myriad non-governmental organizations (NGOs) interested in security issues in the region, very few are interested in military affairs, which they regard as sensitive. In fact, when the present author visited East Africa (Ethiopia, Kenya and Uganda) in the course of the research for this study, many of the NGOs visited advised him against wasting time on searching for data that were not there. However, the reality was different when he visited the likely sources of data. Not only were the data available; there were long historical series.

The media. In countries where the media are interested in defence expenditure and exert sufficient pressure on government, they have often succeeded in forcing the government to make such information available. They did so in Uganda in the case of the purchase of 'junk helicopters' by the defence authorities. Similarly, in Nigeria, the media have been very vocal in their opposition to unusually high levels of military spending when other sectors of the state appear to be neglected.[8] In trying to appear open, the government is forced to present information on the military budget even if the information is likely to provoke debate because of its doubtful nature.

Unfortunately, until lately there has been only minimal media interest in defence matters in Africa generally. Two factors account for this. One is the existence in many African countries of laws prohibiting the unauthorized publication of state materials or state secrets by the media. Many media organizations across the continent have thus avoided publishing materials as 'sensitive' as defence data. The second is a lack of basic knowledge of security issues generally and of defence in particular among media practitioners. Governments have exploited this ignorance to restrict the information they disseminated to those aspects of public expenditure which they themselves wanted to get across to the general public, while the media accepted the figures published on defence without critical comment. This situation is changing in many African countries as the media are becoming more vocal in their criticism of unusually high military spending, especially where it is seen as being at the expense of social sector spending.

One source of demand that is conspicuously absent in many African states is their parliaments. Indeed, one senior military officer indicated

---

[8] 'Budget '98: the loose ends', *The Guardian* (Lagos), 14 Jan. 1998, p. 14.

that, although his country has always had a parliamentary defence committee, the commitment had never vetted any budget submitted by the military. It had never done any major work and only came to life after May 2000 when rebels in Sierra Leone took hostage several members of the forces who were serving with the UN peacekeeping force there. In another parliament, a member of the defence committee confessed that, although the constitution empowered the committee to scrutinize the defence budget and reduce it if necessary, it had hardly ever done so because quite often it was satisfied with the president's justification for it, which were always in the national interest.

Where the local demand factor is not present and there is a reduced capacity for reporting data, it is most probable that data will be difficult to obtain. On the other hand, where all the demand factors are present or there is one powerful one, such as a donor or a large research community in security issues, demand 'pull' is likely to be strong enough to pressure government into providing the data.

What that pull cannot guarantee is the quality of such data.

III. Data quality

Although all the countries examined in this study publish data on military expenditure, it is doubtful whether these data actually represent the full extent of their financial commitments to their military sectors. Moreover, the lack of detail in the data, exemplified by their highly aggregated nature, reduces their value since data are most useful when broken down into their component parts. This is one of the main reasons why users of military expenditure data turn elsewhere for their information. Lack of confidence in official data on military expenditure as published by national governments is responsible for the preference for data from secondary sources, such as SIPRI, shown by many consumers of military expenditure data.[9] Yet all data originate from national governments. Reporting institutions do not have the resources or additional sources of information to enable them to make independent estimates to any great extent. The issue of data quality can only be addressed at source.

---

[9] Brzoska, M., 'The reporting of military expenditures', *Journal of Peace Research*, vol. 18, no. 3 (1981), pp. 261–75.

There are two issues involved in data quality: reliability and validity. Reliability concerns the accuracy of data and validity concerns their coverage, that is, whether they are a true representation of what they claim to represent.

Data reliability

The problem exists at two levels: (*a*) lack of qualified personnel to perform proper accounts reconciliation, and (*b*) deliberate manipulation of figures.

One important aspect of reduced capacity to compile proper statistics because of loss of qualified personnel is the apparent lack of professionalism in the conduct of state finances. For example, in 1990, Burundi had only one qualified accountant in the whole public sector, while Mali had only six.[10] In Nigeria a great many highly qualified accountants and economists have moved to the better-paying private sector, while the wage structure in the civil service is not competitive enough to attract young and qualified accountants and economists, leaving the public sector bereft of qualified professionals.[11] In such situations, budget preparation and the reconciliation of accounts are left in the hands of unqualified people or even external consultants who have little knowledge of the internal operations of the state.

However, states have also been found to manipulate public expenditure figures deliberately, especially in the field of defence, for their own purposes. These have ranged from the need to deceive donors to satisfying domestic demand for less military spending and more social sector expenditure. This deliberate hiding of the true cost of military spending is now believed to have become almost a normal part of the fiscal operations of many of the states in the study.

This problem has not always existed. It appears that it is a post-1985 phenomenon. Prior to this period, military expenditure data published by national governments in Africa appear to have reflected actual expenditure on defence. Five reasons can be advanced to suggest why this was possible.

---

[10] Makanda, J., *Accounting and Auditing Standards in Sub–Saharan Africa* (World Bank, Capacity Building and Implementation Division, Africa Technical Department: Washington, DC, 1995), p. 27.

[11] This was before 2000. In 2000 public sector wages and salaries were raised considerably by the new civilian administration which came to power in 1999.

1. From independence until the mid-1980s, the structures inherited from the colonial powers was still intact in most African countries. African professionals took over the structures and kept up the system for preparing annual budget estimates and compiling statistics relevant to planning and governance. It was during this period that earlier studies reported on the availability of data on military expenditure in a good number of developing countries, including Africa.

2. This period fell within the cold war era, when military purchases were considered normal and did not need to be hidden.

3. In most African states there was little public interest in the issue of military expenditure at this time.

4. This was the era in which military regimes and one-party states were the norm rather than the exception in Africa, and there was little or no public scrutiny of government finances and thus no need to alter or hide figures to please anyone. African armed forces were also being modernized and the strengthening of the military was considered legitimate, necessary and a sign of nationhood.

5. While donors have always been present in African states, their interest in security issues at this time had nothing to do with the level of spending on the military vis-à-vis other sectors. Their main concern was of an ideological and strategic kind, namely to prevent the other camp from getting a foothold in 'their' country or region of influence. They thus encouraged military build-ups in the countries they favoured and even supplied them with armaments, either by opening lines of credit for some or through direct cash payments.[12]

Before the mid-1980s and until the end of the cold war, there was therefore little need to hide military expenditure figures, although the mass exodus of trained professionals was already taking its toll on both the ability to produce statistics and the quality of the statistics being produced by governments across Africa.

From the mid-1980s the situation changed dramatically as all the factors that had aided the production of accurate and reliable statistics in most African states began to erode rapidly. Qualified professionals were leaving the civil services in large numbers, and replacing them was difficult as the IMF-sponsored structural adjustment programmes (SAPs) being adopted across Africa from the early 1980s not only

---

[12] For details see Clapham, C., *Africa and the International System: The Politics of State Survival* (Cambridge University Press: Cambridge, 1996), chapter 6, especially the section on 'the militarisation of Africa's external relations', pp. 150–59.

emphasized a ceiling on new recruitment but also 'capped' public sector salaries. The civil service was thus left with only those staff who could not find better offers elsewhere, perhaps because of their limited training or ability. This inevitably affected the amount of information published and the quality of government publications, including intra-government data compilation.

The introduction of the SAPs and the unemployment and hardship that accompanied them unleashed a wave of social unrest in many African countries, which on the one hand made increased security spending a necessity and on the other raised public awareness of how government spent public funds. In particular, it raised public interest in government spending on defence. While governments were cutting back on spending in the social sector, mainly health and education, they were increasing security spending in the light of the spiralling public unrest.

This had an effect on various governments' presentation of their annual budgets, especially the defence budgets. Rather than presenting the entire defence budget, some governments now either present only recurrent expenditure on defence or present the 'whole' budget while hiding some portions of it in other line ministries—as has been the case in Uganda and Zimbabwe. An inquiry into corruption in the Uganda Police Force in 1999 found that funds meant for the military were allocated to the police, who then transferred the funds to the military. According to officials, this was done to avoid the scrutiny of donors.[13] The audit report of Uganda's government finances in 2001 found the practice still in use as a means of augmenting military expenditure.[14] In other instances, highly aggregated data on security rather than defence are provided, as was the case in Nigeria for a brief period in the mid-1990s.

Closely related to this was the end of the cold war, which allowed expanded scope for the work of donors, especially the multilateral donors. They could now introduce security concerns of a different kind into the conditions for the disbursement of economic assistance to developing countries.[15] In particular, they began to contrast military

[13] 'Creative accounting in Africa: hidden skills', *The Economist*, 9 Oct. 1999. See also chapter 8 in this volume.
[14] Uganda, *Report and Opinion of the Auditor General to Parliament on the Public Accounts of the Republic of Uganda for the Year ending 30th of June 2001, Vol. 1* (Office of the Auditor General: Kampala, June 2001), p. 155.
[15] Ball, N., 'Transforming security sectors: the IMF and World Bank approaches', *Conflict, Security and Development*, vol. 1, no. 1 (2001), pp. 45–66.

expenditure with development and to try to make a 'reasonable' level of military spending a condition for their lending and support. This was in addition to their demand for regular and timely production of annual budget estimates and compilation of relevant statistics, and it imposed additional pressures on governments to provide military expenditure data that were within an acceptable level.

In order to provide 'politically correct' military spending figures, governments started manipulating figures to suit the whims of the donors. The case of Zimbabwe testifies clearly to this practice.[16] Ghana and Uganda have also been accused of manipulating figures either to meet donors' demands or to avoid their scrutiny of the structure of public expenditure.[17]

Partly as a result of this, it may be argued that the fiscal openness expected as a result of the return to democracy is not being realized. Most parliaments lack the knowledge of military issues that would make a critical assessment of military budgets possible, and thus succumb to executive pressure to pass these budgets without any form of scrutiny. Worse still, sometimes they conspire with the executive to hide defence budgets under other budget heads away from the scrutiny of the public and donors.

Validity of data

Beyond the reliability problem, there is the problem of validity of the data—the coverage of the published military expenditure data. What is their composition? What do they include and what do they exclude? Knowledge of this will help analysis and allow a proper determination of the accuracy of the published data.

Since military expenditure data emanate from government they should accurately represent the total sum spent by governments on their military. This is not always the case. The deliberate hiding of relevant expenditure mentioned above is an aspect of data reliability. The available military expenditure data in nearly all the countries examined in this study reflect only a part of the total sum spent on the military sector. The portion usually reflected is recurrent expenditure,

---

[16] See chapter 1, section I.

[17] On Ghana see 'Ghana "misled" IMF', BBC online, 6 Feb. 2002, URL <http://news.bbc.co.uk/hi/english/business/newsid_1803000/1803198.stm>; and Hutchful, E., *Ghana's Adjustment Experience: The Paradox of Reform* (United Nations Research Institute for Social Development (UNRISD): Geneva, 2002), especially p. 163. On Uganda see note 14.

while capital expenditure (especially the cost of military procurement) is excluded. Other expenses such as military pensions and some military construction have been deliberately moved to other line ministries, which ultimately means that the military expenditure reported is less than actual expenditure. In addition, several states make additional allocations to defence during the course of the budget year over and above what was originally allocated in the national budget. The final expenditure accounts rarely reflect such additional expenses, thus significantly understating the real amount spent on the military.

The problem of loss of qualified personnel is relevant here as well. When budget preparation and the reconciliation of accounts are left in the hands of unqualified people or even external consultants, the consequence is a loss of comprehensive coverage of fiscal operations. Even where a government does not intend deliberately to leave out an aspect of expenditure in its final accounts, the use of incompetent personnel has often resulted in incomplete coverage of all aspects of public sector expenditure. Defence, with all the myths built around it, is more prone than any other aspect of the public sector to receive less-than-total coverage, more because of lack of competence on the part of state officials than because of any deliberate attempt to hide defence figures.

These are general problems that cut across all the countries in this study, making the published data on military expenditure only partially reliable.

The problems associated with validity can be considered under two headings: (*a*) highly aggregated budget categories and coverage, and (*b*) the existence of off-budget spending and other revenue.

Highly aggregated budget categories and coverage

The norm among the countries examined in this study is to provide aggregated data or at best a semi-disaggregated figure, usually divided into current and development expenditure. This kind of semi-disaggregated figure is difficult to interpret and does not help analysis. For military expenditure data to be useful they have to be disaggregated into their basic components, such as personnel, O&M, procurement (including equipment) and R&D, and the share of each category of expenditure in the total defence budget has to be identified. This sort of breakdown is hardly ever provided by African governments. Where it has been provided it has not been consistent over time, raising questions about the coverage or definition of military expenditure for the country.

Constant changes in the designation and structure of the ministry responsible for defence and of the departments and units under it are a related aspect of the difficulty of identifying the coverage of military expenditure data. Sometimes such changes are no more than a mere change of name, but in other cases they can amount to a major change in the definition of military expenditure. A good example is Cameroon, which specifically created a ministry for the armed forces but retained spending on the new ministry at the previous level. Prior to the creation of this ministry, the salaries of civilian staff of the old ministry were included under military expenditure personnel costs. The new ministry thus had more funds for defence, without attracting either public protest or complaints from donors because of the lack of knowledge of the definition that was in use before and of what the change implied.

Is military expenditure the same as the allocation to the ministry responsible for defence or does it exclude the costs of the civilian staff of the ministry? What aspects of defence are funded from the presidency and which from the main budget? Are paramilitary groups funded from the defence budget? (The answer to this question is very clear in the case of some francophone countries: the gendarmeries are financed from the defence budget; but the position is much less clear in the anglophone and other African countries.) Is what is included in defence funding consistent over time? The problem of lack of consistency in the definition or coverage of military expenditure in the countries in this study means that their published data lack validity.

Off-budget spending and other revenue

Some of the countries examined in this study exclude some aspects of their military expenditure from the military budget. These are either included in the other budget lines or not included in the budget outlays at all. The ways by which such off-budget military spending takes place include (although they are not limited to): (a) resorting to supplementary budgets; (b) the use of contingency funds; (c) spending under non-defence budget lines; (d) special access to a favourable exchange rate for external purchases; (e) covering accumulated wages or pension arrears covered under non-defence budget lines or by special allocations; and (*f*) the 'raiding' of other budget heads, especially the social sectors, for defence and materiel procurement that is thus not accounted for in the defence budget.[18]

The unexplainable cost of military construction and equipment in Kenya, which has never been reflected in the defence budget but has nonetheless appeared in the country's *Statistical Yearbook* regularly for years, is a case in point. As explained in chapter 6, if this were added to the published defence expenditure of Kenya then the latter would be at least 85 per cent higher than what is reported annually.

Similarly, there is the issue of extra-budgetary revenue which is used to finance military activities but is not reflected in the annual budgets. Such sources of revenue have been found to be substantial in some cases and even larger than the published military budget in others. They include special funds; war levies; peacekeeping income; income from military businesses, both legal and illegal; donor support for demobilization; and direct financing of the military in the field through the extraction of natural resources and foreign military assistance. They give the military additional income outside the budget for military activities but are never reported as expenditure for the military. For instance, the estimated cost to Nigeria of the Economic Community of West African States (ECOWAS) Monitoring Group (ECOMOG) operation which it initiated and led between 1990 and 1999 was approximately $12 billion, whereas its military expenditure over the same period amounted to under $3 billion in constant 2000 prices. Thus the funding for the operation could not have come from the defence budget, even though it was clearly a military activity. The explanation offered is that the operation was considered a policy matter, and that such policy matters are funded from a special fund in the country's budget.[19] The fund is hardly open to scrutiny. Namibia is another country that has regularly resorted to 'contingency funds' to fund its military activities, especially its involvement in the war in the DRC.[20]

---

[18] For a detailed analysis of off-budget expenditure and revenue see Hendrickson, D. and Ball, N., *Off-budget Military Expenditure and Revenue: Issues and Policy Perspectives for Donors*, Occasional Papers no. 1 (Centre for Security and Development Group, King's College, London: London, Jan. 2002).

[19] Omitoogun, W. and Oduntan, T., 'Budgeting for the military sector in Nigeria', Report submitted as part of the SIPRI/African Security Dialogue and Research (ASDR) Project on the Military Budgeting Process in Africa, Mar. 2003.

[20] Maletsky, C., 'DRC war to draw on contingency funding', *The Namibian*, 27 Apr. 1999, URL <http://www.namibian.com.na/Focus/DRCcrisis/funding.html>. See also 'Namibia:

Funds from UN peacekeeping operations, which constitute a substantial income for some armed forces in Africa, such as Ghana's, are rarely reported as income and thus hardly reflected in the defence budgets.

This variety of ways of adding to the income and expenditure of the military which are never reported by governments shows that the figures that are available from a number of government sources, even if they are reliable, are not valid. They do not reflect the totality of the money invested on the military or their activities.

While efforts are being made to rein in these other sources of income and hidden channels of financing, the fact remains that until each state establishes a proper definition of its military expenditure and adheres to the principles of sound governance, not only in military matters but in the whole public sector, the validity of military expenditure data provided by governments will be suspect.

IV. The trend and level of military expenditure in Africa

In analysing the trend and level of military expenditure in Africa, the questions of reliability and validity discussed above should be borne in mind. In the case of Nigeria in the 1990s, for instance, the official data show the trend as fluctuating and the level as more or less the same throughout the period (with a share of military expenditure in GDP of less than 1 per cent throughout), but if the cost of Nigeria's operations in ECOMOG, the favourable exchange rate the military enjoyed for the most part during the period when it was providing troops for ECOMOG, and the cost of several projects undertaken for the military by the PTF are included, the result is an entirely different trend and a share of GDP much higher than the official data would suggest. Similarly, in the case of Kenya, taking into account the considerable amount of off-budget defence spending identified in this study, the actual trend could well be a sustained increase over the years rather than the decrease since 1990 shown by the official military expenditure data. In a similar vein, the secrecy associated with Ethiopia's military expenditure and the lack of any meaningful

---

Auditor General calls on government to reduce unauthorized spending', *The Namibian*, 28 Sep. 2001, in Foreign Broadcast Information Service, *Daily Report–Africa (FBIS-AFR)*, FBIS-AFR-2001-0928, 1 Oct. 2001.

detail in the defence budget in the 1990s should prescribe caution in analysing the military expenditure trend in the country.

The determinants of military expenditure in the case studies in this book (and by extension on the African continent as a whole) are as diverse as the countries. In most cases these factors are country-specific; in others they are sub-regionally determined. Rarely are they continent-wide. As these studies have indicated, the military expenditure trend in East Africa is dictated more by regional dynamics than by internal factors. In a few countries (such as Uganda), internal and external factors contribute in almost equal proportions to determine the level of military expenditure. In Kenya, the main power of the sub-region, external factors affect the level of military expenditure more than internal factors and also play some role in the manipulation of the true cost of military expenditure. Ethiopia's military expenditure is determined as much by the presence of hostile neighbours, Somalia and Eritrea, as by its domestic politics. In West Africa, however, the internal dynamics are more important than regional factors.

It is thus misleading to talk in terms of factors that determine the military expenditure of Africa in general. Instead, the emphasis should be on country-specific determinants or at best the sub-regional factors that determine military expenditure, as the security interests of states with contiguous borders are inevitably interlinked.

V. Summary and conclusions

This report confirms the findings of earlier studies—that military expenditure data exist in the countries examined here and, by extension, in many African countries. It has also shown that data have been published for many years in the different countries. The availability of data differs between countries, as does their quality. Generally, however, the quality of data has been on the decline in the various countries since the 1980s.

The major problems with the data are those of reliability and validity: they are neither accurate nor fully representative of what they are supposed to represent.

Chief among the factors responsible for these problems is the loss of qualified personnel to compile vital statistics. The massive loss of personnel from various civil services across Africa was a consequence of the deep economic crises experienced by many of the countries, leading to a massive decline in real income for the professionals, who then left. The donors have since realized that this is a major deficiency in many African countries and have begun to support efforts to rebuild the capacities to compile necessary data in the various states.

In the meantime, the problem of data quality has been compounded by deliberate attempts by governments who are dependent on external assistance to hide the true cost of their expenditure on military activity from the donors, who insist on a 'reasonable' level of spending on defence. In other countries where donor influence is minimal, other factors have motivated them to manipulate their data. These include a vocal press and informed citizens who prefer higher social spending to increased military spending. This has prompted a more conscious presentation of the allocation of resources between the state sectors, not necessarily in order to reflect a truly equitable distribution of resources but in order to produce one that appears, at least on paper, to be fair to all sectors. This has been a motive for the production of manipulated data, if not in all sectors at least in the defence sector. The realization by users of military expenditure data—donors, researchers and others—that not all activities that are military are captured by the official military expenditure data gave rise to the suspicion that the data presented about the military in many countries might not be representative of the true cost of the military.

The central question this study has thrown up is: How is it possible to determine the actual level of resources devoted to military activities? In other words, how can we ensure that the data on military expenditure reflect the true costs of military activities? It is a question that impinges on the core of research on military expenditure. It also has very direct implications for the efforts of donor agencies that attempt to keep a lid on the injudicious use of public resources for military activities. How effectively the problem is tackled will have a bearing on the conclusions made on the basis of the available data by analysts and, of course, on the soundness of donor policies aimed at ensuring that states struggling to meet the basic needs of their people do not over-allocate scarce resources to the military sector.

VI. Recommendations

Two principal recommendations can be made to ease the problems identified in the study. They concern: (*a*) increased research into the process of budgeting for defence, including planning and monitoring of approved sums, and (*b*) capacity building in the analysis of military affairs and the compilation of statistics in Africa.

The best way to understand how weak the military expenditure data are may be to carry out further research into African military expenditure, and in particular into how countries decide on their annual military expenditure. A study of the process of budgeting for the military sector should reveal more information on:

- the coverage of military expenditure;
- the rationale behind the level and trend of military expenditure, including the policy guiding allocations to the sector;
- the other determining factors;
- the critical actors and institutions in the process of budgeting for the military;
- the degree of transparency in the process and, by implication, the reliability of the data; and
- the other sources of income open to the military (off-budget sources of finance).

The second possible solution is to enhance the research capacity of African scholars on military affairs and to train more staff for the government departments and organizations involved in compiling statistics. This is important because there is an apparent lack of expertise on security studies generally and military affairs in particular.

Apart from Nigeria and South Africa, very few countries in Africa have local experts in the area of security studies, and in particular on military expenditure. As the case of Nigeria shows, there is no guarantee that the development of a corps of experts will lead to more reliable data being produced, but they can serve as the basis to support institutions and individuals invested with the responsibility for oversight of the military. They will also serve as a watchdog of a sort. In this regard, international development cooperation agencies can play a critical role by organizing courses and supporting local NGOs with proven capacities to train people in the field.

Finally, an important aspect of this capacity-building effort will be the provision of the necessary infrastructure such experts need in order to carry out their tasks effectively and efficiently.

Appendix. Military expenditure and economic data, 1980–2002

Table A1. Cameroon: military expenditure and economic data, 1982–2002[a]

All values in US$ are in constant (2000) prices and exchange rates. Figures in italics are percentages. All percentages are rounded.

| Year | Military expenditure[b] | | CGE[b] | Military exp. as % of CGE | GDP | Military exp. as % of GDP | Aid[c] | CGE | Aid as % of CGE |
	(b. current CFA francs)	(US $m. 2000)	(b. current CFE francs)		(b. current CFA francs)		(US $m. 2000)	(US $m. 2000)	
1982	26	99	453	*5.6*	2 618	*1.1*	356.55	1 762	*20*
1983	31	105	507	*6.2*	3 195	*1.1*	214.82	1 691	*13*
1984	39	115	636	*6.1*	3 896	*1.1*	327.97	1 903	*17*
1985	45	125	814	*5.6*	4 135	*1.2*	269.05	2 246	*12*
1986	50	128	839	*6.0*	3 783	*1.4*	300.02	2 147	*14*
1987	49	110	715	*6.9*	3 579	*1.3*	240.21	1 618	*15*
1988	46	102	615	*7.5*	3 424	*1.3*	301.03	1 369	*22*
1989	47	106	545	*8.6*	3 327	*1.4*	505.73	1 232	*41*
1990	49	110	495	*9.9*	3 247	*1.5*	425.17	1 108	*38*
1991	50	112	537	*9.3*	3 150	*1.6*	491.65	1 200	*41*
1992	49	109	520	*9.4*	3 271	*1.4*	610.98	1 162	*53*
1993	48	110	448	*10.6*	3 786	*1.3*	481.87	1 035	*47*
1994	52	90	478	*11.0*	4 366	*1.3*	642.90	817	*79*
1995	57	89	572	*9.9*	4 837	*1.2*	340.40	897	*38*

1996	60	90	755	7.9	5 267	1.1	326.00	1 139	29
1997	69	100	967	7.1	5 572	1.2	440.77	1 394	32
1998	81	113	1 067	7.6	6 008	1.3	456.00	1 489	31
1999	89	123	1 125	7.9	6 602	1.3	400.82	1 546	26
2000	88	123	1 318	6.6	6 320	1.4	379.94	1 850	21
2001	91	122	1 511	6.0	6 615	1.4	409.58	2 029	20
2002	102	131	1 501	6.8	6 987	1.5	..	1 930	..

CGE = Central government expenditure; CFA = Communauté Financière Africaine; GDP = Gross domestic product.
.. = Not available or not applicable.

[a] Up to 2002, the Cameroonian fiscal year was different from the calendar year. Figures in this table are for calendar years, calculated on the assumption of an even rate of expenditure throughout the fiscal year.

[b] Figures are actual expenditure except those for 2000–2002, which are estimates.

[c] Aid = net overall development assistance from member countries of the Organisation for Economic Co-operation and Development (OECD) Development Assistance Committee (DAC), multilateral agencies and Arab countries to Africa, 1980–2001.

Sources: **Military expenditure and central government expenditure**: Cameroonian Ministry of Economy and Finance, 'Loi de Finances de la République du Cameroun' (Ministry of Economy and Finance: Yaoundé, various years); and 'Public revenue and expenditure of the Republic of Cameroon' (Ministry of Economy and Finance: Yaoundé, undated, c. 2000). **GDP**: *International Financial Statistics* (International Monetary Fund: Washington, DC, monthly and annual, various years). **Aid**: Organisation for Economic Co-operation and Development (OECD) Development Assistance Committee (DAC) database, URL <http://www.oecd.org/dac/stats/>.

Table A2. Ethiopia: military expenditure and economic data, 1981–2002[a]

All values in US$ are in constant (2000) prices and exchange rates. Figures in italics are percentages. All percentages are rounded.

Year	Military expenditure[b]		CGE[b] (m. current birr)	Military exp. as % of CGE	GDP (m. current birr)	Military exp. as % of GDP	Aid[c] (US $m. 2000)	CGE (US $m. 2000)	Aid as % of CGE
	(m. current birr)	US $m. (2000)							
1981	760	267	1 790	*42.5*	10 636	*7.1*	418.57	629	*67*
1982	802	266	1 941	*41.3*	11 775	*6.8*	347.79	644	*54*
1983	845	283	2 134	*39.6*	10 988	*7.7*	607.71	713	*85*
1984	876	270	2 322	*37.7*	13 027	*6.7*	658.58	716	*92*
1985	889	230	2 443	*36.4*	13 575	*6.5*	1 274.47	632	*202*
1986	909	261	2 553	*35.6*	14 391	*6.3*	895.07	733	*122*
1987	987	290	2 868	*34.4*	14 971	*6.6*	755.18	844	*89*
1988	1 273	350	3 428	*37.1*	15 742	*8.1*	1 082.76	942	*115*
1989	1 618	412	3 956	*40.9*	16 826	*9.6*	848.63	1 008	*84*
1990	1 625	393	4 507	*36.1*	19 195	*8.5*	1 005.12	1 092	*92*
1991	1 095	196	5 169	*21.2*	20 792	*5.3*	1 077.93	923	*117*
1992	716	116	5 759	*12.4*	26 671	*2.7*	1 076.31	930	*116*
1993	819	128	7 244	*11.3*	28 329	*2.9*	1 072.80	1 130	*95*
1994	813	118	8 658	*9.4*	33 885	*2.4*	1 000.72	1 255	*80*
1995	754	99	9 162	*8.2*	37 938	*2.0*	761.52	1 208	*63*
1996	803	112	9 800	*8.2*	41 465	*1.9*	705.09	1 361	*52*
1997	1 512	205	10 751	*14.1*	45 034	*3.4*	539.09	1 458	*37*

1998	3 263	431	15 155	21.5	48 422	6.7	613.52	1 739	35
1999	5 589	685	16 067	34.8	51 869	10.8	609.22	1 968	31
2000	5 075	618	16 322	31.1	51 962	9.8	692.97	1 986	35
2001	3 154	418	16 662	18.9	51 158	6.2	1 112.49	2 207	50
2002	3 000	406	18 799	16.0	57 092	5.3	..	2 544	..

CGE = Central government expenditure. GDP = Gross domestic product.

.. = Not available or not applicable.

^{a} The Ethiopian fiscal year is different from the calendar year. Figures in this table are for calendar years, calculated on the assumption of an even rate of expenditure throughout the fiscal year.

^{b} Figures are actual expenditure except those for 2001 and 2002, which are estimates.

^{c} Aid = net overall development assistance from member countries of the Organisation for Economic Co-operation and Development (OECD) Development Assistance Committee (DAC), multilateral agencies and Arab countries to Africa, 1980–2001.

Sources: **Military expenditure and central government expenditure**: Ethiopian Central Statistical Authority, *Statistical Abstract* (Central Statistical Authority: Addis Ababa, various years); and National Bank of Ethiopia, *Annual Report* (National Bank of Ethiopia: Addis Ababa, various years). **GDP**: *International Financial Statistics* (International Monetary Fund: Washington, DC, monthly and annual, various years). **Aid**: Organisation for Economic Co-operation and Development (OECD) Development Assistance Committee (DAC) database, URL <http://www.oecd.org/dac/stats/>.

Table A3. Ghana: military expenditure and economic data, 1983–2002

All values in US$ are in constant (2000) prices and exchange rates. Figures in italics are percentages. All percentages are rounded.

Year	Military expenditure[a]		CGE (m. current cedis)	Military exp. as % of CGE	GDP (m. current cedis)	Military exp. as % of GDP	Aid[b] (US $m. 2000)	CGE (US $m. 2000)	Aid as % of CGE
	(m. current cedis)	(US $m. 2000)							
1983	..	..	14 755	..	184 038	*8.0*	197.40	160	*123*
1984	1 605	13	26 691	*6.0*	270 561	*0.6*	388.55	207	*188*
1985	3 432	24	45 764	*7.5*	343 048	*1.0*	367.43	322	*114*
1986	4 605	26	70 659	*6.5*	511 000	*0.9*	535.17	400	*134*
1987	6 659	27	102 135	*6.5*	746 000	*0.9*	524.28	413	*127*
1988	4 603	14	143 897	*3.2*	1 051 000	*0.4*	677.87	443	*153*
1989	6 106	15	196 466	*3.1*	1 417 000	*0.4*	859.92	483	*178*
1990	9 006	16	254 473	*3.5*	2 032 000	*0.4*	601.14	456	*132*
1991	15 230	23	340 262	*4.5*	2 575 000	*0.6*	904.59	516	*175*
1992	18 201	25	498 813	*3.6*	3 008 800	*0.6*	589.91	688	*86*
1993	26 600	29	760 911	*3.5*	3 674 900	*0.7*	611.59	840	*73*
1994	36 147	32	1 141 313	*3.2*	5 204 800	*0.7*	516.60	1 000	*52*
1995	58 823	33	1 698 700	*3.5*	7 751 700	*0.8*	556.36	941	*59*
1996	72 644	28	2 543 100	*2.9*	11 338 700	*0.6*	572.61	962	*60*
1997	93 148	28	3 764 200	*2.5*	14 113 400	*0.7*	470.95	1 113	*42*
1998	132 812	34	4 383 200	*3.0*	17 296 000	*0.8*	699.62	1 342	*52*
1999	158 060	36	5 845 500	*2.7*	20 580 000	*0.8*	584.50	1 278	*46*

2000	277 269	51	6 972 000	4.0	27 153 000	1.0	609.39	1 372	44
2001	231 740	32	9 945 000	2.3	38 014 000	0.6	666.57	1 542	43
2002	..	..	12 799 000	..	..	..	..	..	..

CGE = Central government expenditure. GDP = Gross domestic product.
.. = Not available or not applicable.

[a] Figures are actual expenditure except those for 2001 and 2002, which are estimates.
[b] Aid = net overall development assistance from member countries of the Organisation for Economic Co-operation and Development (OECD) Development Assistance Committee (DAC), multilateral agencies and Arab countries to Africa, 1980–2001.

Sources: **Military expenditure 1984–85 and 1987**: *Government Finance Statistics Yearbook* (International Monetary Fund: Washington, DC, various years). **Military expenditure 1986 and 1988–95**: Ghanaian Statistical Service, *Quarterly Digest of Statistics* (Ghanaian Statistical Service: Accra, various editions). **Military expenditure 1996–97**: Ghanaian Statistical Service, response to questionnaire; **Military expenditure 1998–2000**: Ghanaian Parliament, *Parliamentary Debates: Official Report* (Graphic Corporation and Department of Official Report: Accra, various years). **Central government expenditure 1983–2000**: Ghanaian Statistical Service, *Quarterly Digest of Statistics* (Ghanaian Statistical Service: Accra, various editions). **Military expenditure and central government expenditure 2001 and 2002**: International Monetary Fund, IMF Country Report no. 02/38 (IMF: Washington, DC, Mar. 2002). **GDP**: *International Financial Statistics* (International Monetary Fund: Washington, DC, monthly and annual, various years). **Aid**: Organisation for Economic Co-operation and Development (OECD) Development Assistance Committee (DAC) database, URL <http://www.oecd.org/dac/stats/>.

Table A4. Kenya: military expenditure and economic data, 1981–2002[a]
All values in US$ are in constant (2000) prices and exchange rates. Figures in italics are percentages. All percentages are rounded.

Year	Military expenditure[b] (m. current shillings)	Military expenditure[b] (US $m. 2000)	CGE[b] (m. current shillings)	Military exp. as % of CGE	GDP (m. current shillings)	Military exp. as % of GDP	Aid[c] (US $m. 2000)	CGE (US $m. 2000)	Aid as % of CGE
1981	2 206	332	20 943	*10.5*	51 641	*4.3*	754.63	3 154	*24*
1982	2 689	336	23 133	*11.6*	58 214	*4.6*	830.12	2 887	*29*
1983	2 778	311	24 335	*11.4*	66 218	*4.2*	714.96	2 726	*26*
1984	2 523	256	27 257	*9.3*	72 550	*3.5*	747.45	2 769	*27*
1985	2 396	215	31 117	*7.7*	100 831	*2.4*	770.64	2 797	*28*
1986	2 941	252	36 915	*8.0*	117 472	*2.5*	641.96	3 166	*20*
1987	4 111	328	42 620	*9.6*	131 169	*3.1*	688.11	3 397	*20*
1988	4 454	319	53 747	*8.3*	151 194	*2.9*	968.89	3 852	*25*
1989	4 703	298	63 928	*7.4*	171 589	*2.7*	1 258.50	4 057	*31*
1990	5 648	310	72 406	*7.8*	195 536	*2.9*	1 231.55	3 975	*31*
1991	5 279	242	83 904	*6.3*	221 250	*2.4*	956.99	3 844	*25*
1992	5 027	178	105 383	*4.8*	264 967	*1.9*	844.77	3 725	*23*
1993	6 131	149	151 747	*4.0*	333 613	*1.8*	890.41	3 681	*24*
1994	6 577	124	172 887	*3.8*	400 722	*1.6*	632.37	3 251	*19*
1995	7 668	143	174 610	*4.4*	465 653	*1.6*	620.46	3 257	*19*
1996	9 756	167	183 670	*5.3*	527 967	*1.8*	518.50	3 146	*16*
1997	10 327	159	249 440	*4.1*	623 354	*1.7*	419.66	3 839	*11*

1998	10 381	150	278 941	*3.7*	692 120	*1.5*	395.87	4 024	*10*
1999	10 503	146	233 192	*4.5*	748 925	*1.4*	296.58	3 251	*9*
2000	12 347	162	275 527	*4.5*	788 917	*1.6*	512.14	3 617	*14*
2001	14 948	195	278 485	*5.4*	825 000	*1.8*	466.27	3 628	*13*
2002	15 835	200	238 491	*6.6*	877 000	*1.8*	..	3 006	*..*

a The Kenyan fiscal year runs from 1 June of the named year. Figures in this table are for calendar years, calculated on the assumption of an even rate of expenditure throughout the fiscal year.

b Figures are actual expenditure except those for 1998–2002, which are estimates.

c Aid = net overall development assistance from member countries of the Organisation for Economic Co-operation and Development (OECD) Development Assistance Committee (DAC), multilateral agencies and Arab countries to Africa, 1980–2001.

CGE = Central government expenditure. GDP = Gross domestic product.

.. = Not available or not applicable.

Sources: **Military expenditure and central government expenditure except 2001 and 2002**: Kenyan Central Bureau of Statistics, *Statistical Abstract* (Central Bureau of Statistics: Nairobi, various years); and *Economic Survey* (Nairobi, various years). **Military expenditure and central government expenditure 2001 and 2002**: Kenyan Government, 'Interim poverty reduction strategy paper, 2002–2003', Kenyan Government, Nairobi, 2000, annex 5. **GDP**: *International Financial Statistics* (International Monetary Fund: Washington, DC, monthly and annual, various issues). **Aid**: Organisation for Economic Co-operation and Development (OECD) Development Assistance Committee (DAC) database, URL <http://www.oecd.org/dac/stats/>.

Table A5. Nigeria: military expenditure and economic data, 1980–2002

All values in US$ are in constant (2000) prices and exchange rates. Figures in italics are percentages. All percentages are rounded.

Year	Military expenditure[a] (m. current naira)	Military expenditure[a] (US $m. 2000)	CGE[a] (m. current naira)	Military exp. as % of CGE	GDP (m current naira)	Military exp. as % of GDP	Aid[b] (US $m. 2000)	CGE (US $m. 2000)	Aid as % of CGE
1980	780	699	14 969	*5.2*	50 270	*1.6*	54.82	13 412	*0.41*
1981	821	609	11 414	*7.2*	50 751	*1.6*	68.99	8 465	*0.82*
1982	745	513	11 923	*6.2*	51 953	*1.4*	67.92	8 211	*0.83*
1983	1 101	615	9 637	*11.4*	57 144	*1.9*	98.96	5 386	*1.84*
1984	920	368	9 928	*9.3*	63 608	*1.4*	62.10	3 975	*1.56*
1985	976	364	13 041	*7.5*	72 355	*1.3*	61.21	4 860	*1.26*
1986	907	320	16 224	*5.6*	73 062	*1.2*	88.65	5 720	*1.55*
1987	810	257	22 019	*3.7*	108 885	*0.7*	87.41	6 975	*1.25*
1988	1 230	252	27 750	*4.4*	145 243	*0.8*	143.20	5 689	*2.52*
1989	1 257	171	41 028	*3.1*	224 797	*0.6*	447.03	5 590	*8.00*
1990	2 229	283	60 268	*3.7*	260 637	*0.9*	293.33	7 649	*3.83*
1991	2 415	425	66 584	*3.6*	328 115	*0.7*	268.59	7 208	*3.73*
1992	3 004	233	92 797	*3.2*	620 077	*0.5*	252.89	9 450	*2.68*
1993	6 382	315	191 229	*3.3*	967 280	*0.7*	278.46	5 063	*5.50*
1994	7 032	221	160 893	*4.4*	1 237 122	*0.6*	178.83	4 439	*4.03*
1995	14 000	255	243 768	*5.7*	1 977 740	*0.7*	180.55	4 058	*4.45*
1996	15 353	216	288 095	*5.3*	2 824 000	*0.5*	167.75	5 574	*3.01*

1997	17 920	233	428 215	4.2	2 940 000	0.6	191.09	5 749	3.32
1998	25 162	273	487 113	5.2	2 838 000	0.9	194.46	10 673	1.82
1999	45 400	511	947 690	4.8	3 320 000	1.4	145.03	6 893	2.10
2000	37 490	369	701 059	5.3	4 981 000	0.8	184.83	8 862	2.09
2001	63 472	553	1 018 025	6.2	5 640 000	1.1	189.34	7 909	2.39
2002	64 908	483	1 064 801	6.1	..	..	..	..	..

CGE = Central government expenditure. GDP = Gross domestic product.

.. = Not available or not applicable.

^a Figures prior to 1985 are actual expenditure. All others are revised figures and estimates. All known supplementary allocations have been included.

^b Aid = net overall development assistance from member countries of the Organisation for Economic Co-operation and Development (OECD) Development Assistance Committee (DAC), multilateral agencies and Arab countries to Africa, 1980–2001.

Sources: **Military expenditure and central government expenditure**: Central Bank of Nigeria, *Statistical Bulletin: Government Finance Statistics*, vol. 12 (Dec. 2002); Central Bank of Nigeria, *Annual Report* (Central Bank of Nigeria: Abuja, 1999, 2000, 2001); and Nigerian National Assembly, Senate, 2002 Appropriation Bill, Abuja, Mar. 2002. **GDP**: *International Financial Statistics* (International Monetary Fund: Washington, DC, monthly and annual, various years). **Aid**: Organisation for Economic Co-operation and Development (OECD) Development Assistance Committee (DAC) database, URL <http://www.oecd.org/dac/stats/>.

Table A6. Uganda: military expenditure and economic data, 1983–2002[a]

All values in US$ are in constant (2000) prices and exchange rates. Figures in italics are percentages. All percentages are rounded.

Year	Military expenditure[b] (m. current shillings)	Military expenditure[b] (US $m. 2000)	CGE[b] (m. current shillings)	Military exp. as % of CGE	GDP (m. current shillings)	Military exp. as % of GDP	Aid[c] (US $m. 2000)	CGE (US $m. 2000)	Aid as % of CGE
1983	142	49	739	*19.2*	6 142	*2.3*	247.76	255	*97*
1984	289	70	1 069	*27.0*	9 598	*3.0*	305.31	258	*118*
1985	723	68	3 490	*20.7*	25 622	*2.8*	335.98	327	*103*
1986	1 837	66	7 554	*24.3*	65 444	*2.8*	279.13	271	*103*
1987	5 613	67	26 761	*21.0*	224 041	*2.5*	375.37	320	*117*
1988	14 597	59	56 841	*25.7*	634 634	*2.3*	462.38	230	*201*
1989	29 760	75	119 844	*24.8*	1 178 185	*2.5*	533.67	300	*178*
1990	47 926	90	215 263	*22.3*	1 602 094	*3.0*	693.02	405	*171*
1991	56 530	83	335 785	*16.8*	2 222 861	*2.5*	667.45	493	*135*
1992	57 918	56	564 324	*10.3*	3 687 704	*1.6*	671.21	544	*123*
1993	69 799	63	784 894	*8.9*	4 024 186	*1.7*	603.90	713	*85*
1994	95 758	79	884 035	*10.8*	5 171 744	*1.9*	713.99	732	*98*
1995	11 7975	90	988 312	*11.9*	5 977 762	*2.0*	713.75	753	*95*
1996	135 200	96	1 081 000	*12.5*	6 636 521	*2.0*	588.10	769	*76*
1997	138 579	92	1 161 000	*11.9*	7 197 000	*1.9*	758.65	772	*98*
1998	180 550	120	1 360 000	*13.3*	7 799 000	*2.3*	611.94	905	*68*
1999	211 955	133	1 685 500	*12.6*	8 474 000	*2.5*	556.83	1 054	*53*

2000	202 810	123	1 994 500	10.2	9 406 000	2.2	819.45	1 213	68
2001	213 605	127	2 293 000	9.3	10 287 000	2.1	801.59	1 367	59
2002	254 930	152	2 564 500	10.0	11 098 000	2.3	..	1 560	..

a The Ugandan fiscal year runs from Apr. to Mar. Figures are for calendar years, calculated on the assumption of an even rate of expenditure throughout the fiscal year.

b Figures are actual expenditure up to and including 2000.

c Aid = net overall development assistance from member countries of the Organisation for Economic Co-operation and Development (OECD) Development Assistance Committee (DAC), multilateral agencies and Arab countries to Africa, 1980–2001.

CGE = Central government expenditure. GDP = Gross domestic product.

.. = Not available or not applicable.

Sources: **Military expenditure and central government expenditure**: Ugandan Ministry of Finance, Planning and Economic Development; *Background to the Budget* (Ministry of Finance, Planning and Economic Development: Kampala, various years). **GDP**: *Government Finance Statistics Yearbook* (International Monetary Fund: Washington, DC, various years); and *International Financial Statistics* (International Monetary Fund: Washington, DC, monthly and annual, various years). **Aid**: Organisation for Economic Co-operation and Development (OECD) Development Assistance Committee (DAC) database, URL <http://www.oecd.org/dac/stats/>.

Index